THE LAW OF TWO CHILD NORM IN PANCHAYATS

About the Institution

Mahila Chetna Manch (MCM), a Madhya Pradesh based development organization, is working for socio-economic and political empowerment of women. As a facilitator to the process of empowerment, it combines action and research on women issues. MCM has undertaken a number of research studies, including women's entry and experience in panchayats after the 73rd Constitutional Amendment, panchayat finance, gender and governance, gender budgeting, women's access and use of micro-credit, particularly from the Rashtriya Mahila Kosh, the national credit fund especially set up for women. It has studied factors of maternal mortality and is currently engaged in a study of consequences of domestic violence on reproductive health of women. MCM has also conducted a study on child labour in urban informal sector in Bhopal.

About the Author

Mrs. Nirmala Buch, a former officer of Indian Administrative Service has been Secretary to the Government of India in the Ministry of Rural Development, Chief Secretary of Madhya Pradesh and Vice Chairperson of the National Environmental Appellate Authority. At present, she is President of the Mahila Chetna Manch, Bhopal and a visiting fellow in the Centre for Women's Development Studies, New Delhi.

She did her post-graduation in English from Banaras Hindu University and was a Parvin Fellow in Woodrow Wilson School of Public Affairs, Princeton University, USA. She is widely travelled and represented India in various delegations to world conferences and meets on issues of women. She has written extensively on issues of governance, public administration, the functioning of Panchayat Raj and empowerment of women.

The Law of Two Child Norm in Panchayats

Nirmala Buch

in collaboration with

MAHILA CHETNA MANCH, BHOPAL

and

CONCEPT PUBLISHING COMPANY, NEW DELHI-110059

Cataloging in Publication Data—DK
Courtesy: D.K. Agencies (P) Ltd. <docinfo@dkagencies.com>

Buch, Nirmala.
The law of two child norm in panchayats / Nirmala Buch.
p. cm.
In Indian context.
Includes bibliographical references (p.)
Includes index.
ISBN 8180692612

1. Panchayat—India. 2. Local government—Law and legislation—India. 3. Political candidates—Legal status, laws, etc.—India. 4. Birth control—Law and legislation—India. I. Title.

DDC 342.540 9 22

ISBN 81-8069-261-2

First Published 2006

Published and Printed by
Ashok Kumar Mittal
Concept Publishing Company
A/15-16, Commercial Block, Mohan Garden
New Delhi (INDIA)

Phones : 25351460, 25351794
Fax : 091-11-25357103
Email : publishing@conceptpub.com

Preface

India started its Family Planning programme in 1952. Since then it was rechristened as family welfare programme and moved from a target based programme with incentives, disincentives and 'population control' to 'population stabilization'. The country signed CEDAW, ICPD Cairo Programme of Action 1994, and formulated a National Policy for Empowerment of Women, and a National Population Policy. Constitutional Amendments in 1992 brought women and weaker sections and youth in the rural and urban local bodies and then another Amendment in 2002 mandated universal elementary education to all children aged 6-14 years. These initiatives and national and international commitments were following the vision of the Constitution of India guaranteeing to all citizens, justice, liberty and equality enshrined in the Fundamental Rights and Directive Principles of State Policy.

Policies and programmes of the Indian Republic must be critiqued in this light and any measure that does not pass this test must be reviewed. It is with this approach that this volume looks at the law of two-child norm introduced in panchayats in some of the states, which disqualifies persons from entering or remaining in panchayats if they have more than two children after a specified date. This measure seeks to compel them to take fertility decisions in compliance of this limit and set example for others, but is hopelessly out of tune with the national and international discourse which, taking note of the past experience of the futility of coercive methods, gives centrality to women's autonomy and agency, overall and social development and responsible choice of individuals in population policies and population stabilisation.

Mahila Chetna Manch and I have been engaged with the Panchayats and have documented the experiences of women in MP, Rajasthan and UP. Our first encounter with the effect of this law in Rajasthan where a young elected woman in Panchayat was compelled to conceal her baby and not even been able to feed her, made it imperative that we look at this law, and its experiences in the six states which had introduced it. The results of our study in the states of AP, Haryana, MP, Orissa and Rajasthan confirm the apprehensions particularly expressed by women's organizations when this law was made in Haryana and Rajasthan.

I have organised the contents in this volume in five chapters. The introduction contains the context of population growth rate in India and the decentralization of governance up to the grassroots level with the 73rd Constitutional Amendment. The two-child norm must be understood in this context. Ignoring this context of a major initiative of bringing the earlier politically, socially and economically marginalised sections in a critical number to participate in grassroots democracy results in designing tools for addressing the concern about population growth rates, which can adversely affect the presence and participation of these very sections. The second chapter presents the details of the study on which this volume is based, the rationale, objectives, methodology and the areas of operation of the study and the procedure of data collection.

The third chapter provides the details of the experiences as narrated by the Panchayat representatives affected by the implementation of the two-child norm law. The analysis of the consequences of the two-child norm law and the perspectives and opinions of policy makers, media persons, lawyers, NGOs engaged with the issues of Panchayats and gender in these states and the judicial pronouncements are also presented here. The fourth chapter presents case studies which reveal the major implications of a two-child norm law for men and women who have not been able to meet the conditionalities of this law and have adopted practices to try to show compliance. The last chapter presents analysis of the results of the study and emerging issues. Our field data and experience of the norm in five of the six states which had introduced this law in panchayats till 2001 shows the practices and consequences which are adverse for women and girl children. Its consequence on weaker sections entering panchayats after reservations, are aggravated with the combination of power politics and use of law against new aspirants. The voices of those adversely affected by this law make a clear case for immediate review of this measure and wider discussions on the issues involved. It is also seen that in large sections of the population, the desire for a small family exists independent of such a law. This has to be supported by steps to ensure women's autonomy and agency, and social development and the state focusing on ensuring quality health care and contraceptive services in all areas and to all population groups.

This is the age of impact assessments of projects and programmes. It is time that all measures and laws, however attractive they appear, e.g. to reduce population growth rate, are subjected to public scrutiny not only about their contribution to fulfilling some of the stated objectives but also about any unintended negative implications for the disadvantaged and for women before these are adopted. As most of such measures are in the jurisdiction of the states, conventions may be evolved to have a national debate and consensus before individual states introduce them.

Nirmala Buch

Acknowledgements

I am grateful to UNFPA, New Delhi who supported the research on which this book is based. My thanks are to the Mahila Chetna Manch team—M.L. Sharma, Anju, Sangeeta and their colleagues whose tireless work in the field enabled us to capture the experiences and narratives of panchayat representatives. This work could not have been completed without constant push from my husband Mahesh. The discussions and final checks by Dr. Udai Jain, were indispensable and his help is gratefully acknowledged. My thanks to Annapoorna for painstakingly processing the manuscript. My warm, sincere thanks to our respondents in the study who made this publication possible. I hope I have been able to present their case for a much needed debate.

Contents

1

Introduction

The decade of 1990s started with two major developments, first, in democratic decentralisation and second, in population policy and strategies in India. The first related to the conclusion of a major exercise in 1992 with the 73rd Constitutional Amendment mandating regularly elected and more inclusive Panchayats with reservations for the scheduled castes, scheduled tribes and women and lowering of the minimum age for entry to 21 years. The second development was the State's response to the population figures of the 1991 Census, in the conception of a two-child norm for the elected representatives.

Our engagement with Panchayats and particularly with women who entered these institutions in a critical number after the 73rd Constitutional Amendment of 1992 started with the first generation of women representatives who entered these bodies in the Panchayat elections in 1994-95. A Centre for Women's Development Studies (CWDS) report[1] on the experiences of women in Panchayats in MP, Rajasthan and UP, in which the Mahila Chetna Manch was a partner, noted how a woman respondent in Rajasthan had to conceal her infant and was not even able to feed it lest it was identified as her offspring. This drew our attention to the serious implications of the two-child norm which had been introduced through the post-Amendment Panchayat laws in some of the States.

The "two-child norm" for the elected Panchayat representatives runs counter to the objective of bringing women, weaker sections and younger members in these institutions. Hence, the law to empower them is seen as "being circumvented by these imaginatively anti-democratic population policies." (Mohan Rao: 2003). The Mahila Chetna Manch took up in 2001-2002 an exploratory study[2] of this norm in five States—Andhra Pradesh, Haryana, Madhya Pradesh, Orissa and Rajasthan—supported by the UNFPA, which gave us an opportunity to explore the issues involved in the application of this norm in Panchayats. We continued to look at the issue particularly in two of these five States, namely, Madhya Pradesh and Rajasthan, where we are engaged with women in Panchayats and their networks and capacity building and empowering processes.

Our fieldwork in the study of this norm faced the problem of lack of state-level data even about persons affected by the formal legal proceedings in the implementation of this law in Panchayats. Our subsequent follow-up and data collection about the total number of persons affected by this law in various districts of the concerned states has helped in an analysis of its implications further. This monograph is based on our study of the Two-Child Norm in Panchayats in the five states in 2001-2002. We have supplemented it with these subsequent data indicating its analysis separately at appropriate places.

The Context

Village Panchayats were recognised as units of self-government in Article 40 of the Indian Constitution. Several committees later suggested a three-tier system of Panchayats at village, district and intermediate levels.[3] The 73rd Amendment strengthened them further by mandating a more inclusive composition with reservations for women and weaker sections, regular elections and powers and functions throughout the country. As the subject of local self-government is in the jurisdiction of the states in the Constitution, the states were expected to bring their state Panchayat laws in conformity with the Constitutional Amendment within a year. The states of Andhra Pradesh, Haryana, Orissa and Rajasthan introduced the two-child norm in these new Panchayat laws. Madhya Pradesh and Himachal Pradesh followed with similar additions in 2000.

India is well known as the first country in the world to have adopted a Family Planning programme in 1952 as a result of a concern for India's growing population. Beginning from those early days India's Family Planning programme has had a long history. In 1994 India was signatory to the Programme of Action of the International Conference on Population and Development in Cairo (ICPD) which emphasised the relationship between population, sustainable development, comprehensive reproductive health services of good quality, gender equality and the right of individuals and couples to freely and responsibly decide on the number and spacing of their children. This was followed in 1996 by the withdrawal of centrally determined family planning targets, which reversed the trend of a target-driven approach. This change in approach was consolidated by the announcement of the Reproductive and Child Health Programme in 1998 and was given its ultimate shape by the National Population Policy in 2000 (NPP 2000).

The overall vision of the NPP is to ensure social and economic development and improve the quality of life of the people, to enhance their well-being, and to provide them with opportunities and choices to become productive assets in society. It sees the relationship between population and development as a balance between the requirements of sustainable economic growth, social development and environmental protection. This balance is to be achieved through population stabilisation. The NPP provides a very clear explanation of the relationship between population and development, which includes other parameters like comprehensive reproductive health services, education, decentralisation, women's empowerment and so on. This is in consonance with the constitutional promises of the Directive Principles of State Policy. Two other social development policies namely, the National Policy for the Empowerment of Women 2001 and the National Health Policy 2002, reinforced this emphasis on women's empowerment and social development as a key to the success of national development.

The 73rd and 74th Constitutional Amendments in 1992 mandating increased participation of women and weaker sections in Panchayats and urban local bodies and greater decentralisation in local governance and the 93rd Constitutional Amendment for ensuring universal elementary education are the other important milestones in the journey towards realization of the promises made by the founding fathers to the people of India. The constitutional provisions and policies also provide guidelines to examine the policies, programmes and their rules of implementation. Here we look at the two-child norm in Panchayats and its implications and consequences on this understanding. While all the state laws have not specifically stated, the norm seeks to promote contraception and limiting the family size of the entrants to Panchayats and expects their example to be followed by others in the rural society, thus contributing to the overall goal of population stabilization.

Democratic Decentralisation, Panchayats and the Two-Child Norm

The need of democratic decentralisation was inherent in Article 40 of the Constitution of India, which expected the state to constitute Village Panchayats and to endow them with powers and authority, as may be necessary, to enable them to function as units of self-government. Village Panchayats as statutory bodies with municipal and petty dispute resolution functions had been created since the beginning of the twentieth century. In independent India the progress in constituting and sustaining Village Panchayats as units of self-government was uneven across time and states in terms of broad-based participation of all sections of society and powers, authority and resources given to them to perform their expected role.

The decade of the 1980s saw the beginnings of the exercise for a Constitutional Amendment to give a constitutional guarantee for Panchayats throughout the country. In 1988 the 64th Amendment Bill could not be passed in the Parliament. But there were new amendment bills on the subject framed during the National Front Government in 1990 and then the new Congress Government in 1991. Finally, the latest amendment bill including reservations for women and weaker sections and enhanced powers of these bodies and mandating their regular elections, etc., was passed in 1992. It was already before a joint select committee of

Parliament when the first moves for stipulating the restrictions of the two-child norm in Panchayats were made. The irony of introducing the two-child norm in Panchayats just when the earlier politically and socially marginalised sections were given reservations of seats in these grassroots bodies for a more inclusive composition and wider participation is difficult to ignore.

The history of the two-child norm in Panchayats starts after the results of the 1991 Census started coming in and the planners and policy-makers focussed once again on the issue of population growth. In 1992 the National Development Council (NDC) set up a Committee on Population under the chairmanship of the then Chief Minister of Kerala. It recommended that legislation should be brought up in Parliament prohibiting persons with more than two children from holding any post from the Panchayat to Parliament in future. It was suggested that such legislation would convey the country's seriousness about adopting the small-family norm. The report was presented to the NDC in 1993. Though the Chief Minister of Kerala led the committee, Kerala, possibly owing to its background of social development, did not adopt the two-child norm. Instead, it focused on improving health services and education. The norm was not introduced at the national level either. While the national-level debate on the two-child norm has continued inconclusively, a number of states have adopted this norm for the elected representatives in Panchayats. It has also been introduced in urban local bodies and in some states even in other elected bodies such as cooperatives and agricultural produce market committees, etc. and also for entry and promotions of employees in public services and access to government's welfare programmes and services.

Rajasthan was the pioneer in introducing this norm for Panchayats and municipalities in 1992. The states of Andhra Pradesh and Haryana opted for this norm in 1993 for holding elected posts in Panchayats. Orissa introduced it for Zila Parishads in 1993 and for Village and Block Panchayats in 1994. Himachal Pradesh and Madhya Pradesh adopted it in 2000 and Maharashtra in 2003 with retrospective effect from 21st September, 2002. Since the state of Chhattisgarh was created out of Madhya Pradesh in 2001, it also inherited the Panchayat law of Madhya Pradesh with this provision and though it has made some changes in its Panchayat law thereafter, it has chosen to retain the two-child norm so far. Thus while the Committee on Population came up with its recommendation on the two-child norm in 1993, the states introduced the norm over a period from 1992 to 2000. The NDC recommendation of the two child-norm predates the ICPD agreement of 1994 and the National Population Policy. Most of the states adopting the norm (except Madhya Pradesh, Himachal Pradesh and now Maharashtra) have done so before the National Population Policy of 2000.

Population and Development: An Essential Relationship

The relationship between population and development has been a subject matter of debate where one group of experts argued that the number of people was a disadvantage while others argued that productive people were a resource for the country. After the Second World War when the population of many countries in Europe had been severely reduced by war casualties, countries provided incentives to couples to have more children because there were not enough hands to run the economy.

The concept of development too has undergone many changes since the time when development was measured in terms of a country's Gross Domestic Product (GDP) that too measured in US dollar terms. While economic development is still considered important, other parameters have also been included. The United Nations Development Programme (UNDP) introduced the concept of Human Development Index in 1992-93 through its Human Development report with human development including quality of life measured through education and health attainments. Later, gender equality was included as a parameter of human development and the concept of Gender Development Index (GDI) was introduced. The ideas inherent in these concepts are integral to the many provisions of the Indian Constitution notably the Fundamental Rights and Directive Principles of State Policy.

At the international level the consensus understanding of the linkage between population and development was defined at the International Conference on Population and Development at Cairo in 1994. Empowering women and providing them with more choices through expanded access to education and health services and promoting skill development and employment are key features of this new approach. Advocating universal availability of family planning services, the Programme of Action adopted at ICPD 1994 sets down clear goals relating to different aspects of population, development and reproductive health. The National Population Policy, 2000 reiterates the same understanding.

Understanding the Two-Child Norm

The family planning programme has for long promoted the concept of a small family which was epitomised by certain key slogans. Early on, the slogan was *"Do ya teen bachche rehte hein ghar mein achhe"* (two or three kids are good for the home), *"Do ya teen bachche bus"* (only two or three children) which later became *"hum do hamare do"* (we two and ours two). These slogans reflected the current thinking about what should be the ideal number of children in one family but this was not enforced through any legal measure. These slogans, however, almost made a small family equivalent to a Two-Child Family in the public mind as well as among the policy makers. This explains the introduction of a "Two-Child Norm" in public policy as reflected in the rules for public servants and employees in the organised sector and then in the elected bodies and development programmes. Further, and unfortunately, the posters and pictures with these slogans showing a boy with shorts and shirt and a girl in a frock with two plaits also painted a designer family and unwittingly reinforced the son desire with the inclusion of at least one son since the girl was in any case not a preferred choice. Such a designer family can be planned only by adopting questionable measures for limiting the family size along with the choice of sex of the child.

The two-child norm as formulated for disqualification of aspirants to elected posts in Panchayats has the following components: (i) A person will not be eligible for entry or continuance in Panchayats if he or she has more than two children/ more than two living children on and after a specified date,

(ii) Having more than two children does not attract disqualification on the date of coming into effect of the law introducing this disqualification or up to the end of one year of such a date if an additional child is not born thereafter. This formulation in all the laws gives one year's time to comply with the law after it comes into effect. It has consequences for younger aspirants in the reproductive age group.

While Panchayat laws of the states of Andhra Pradesh, Orissa and Rajasthan speak of disqualification of a person if he has more than two children, Haryana and Madhya Pradesh laws speak of disqualification if there are more than two living children. The action to disqualify is taken on a complaint/petition received alleging violation of the norm. The competent authorities are generally the executive officers—Collectors, Commissioners except in Andhra Pradesh and Orissa (for block and district levels) where the judicial officers namely, Munsifs do this adjudication.

The sudden introduction of this norm and the widespread fascination for it draw inspiration from the Chinese one-child policy. China has achieved a remarkable success in reducing its population growth rate, which is supposed to be on the basis of norm-based population policies, and many in India have envied it. In fact during our field study, a number of policy-makers, doctors and others referred to China with obvious admiration. They represent the approach of taking direct control of birth decisions of families through authoritarian intervention, seeing the family's decisions "as either seriously undisciplined or incurably biased, and often very wrong for the society as a whole and perhaps even for the respective families themselves" (Sen, 1995). In China, "raising of the population problem insistently since the announcement of the one-child policy in 1978 produced "willed consent for a strong centralised state" and an "apparent hegemonic status of the one-child policy, perhaps the most stringent population policy in the world history" (Ann Anagnost, 1995). The norm was universally applied in China but not through a law till very recently and was enforced primarily through recognition, rewards and disincentives and the pressure for compliance from the loyal party cadres.

Data show that fertility decline in China had begun even before the one-child policy was enforced. "In its grave demographic distortion of the Chinese population and in the pain it produces, this policy appears as a monumental form of national self-mutilation" (Ann Anagnost, 1995). The negative implication of the one-child policy was seen in China in "gendered social problems, frightful in nature and proportion", and "worrying socio-demographic consequences" (Greenhalgh, 2001) of declining child sex ratio and the reducing number of girl children, so relaxations were made in the policy, which was loosened further, and took son preference into greater account. Many rural communities moved to institute a two-child policy and adopted an exception allowing couples whose first child was a girl to have a second child. (ZengYi, 1989, Short *et al.*, 1998).

The assumption in introducing a government enforced norm for restricting the number of children is that it will encourage couples to adopt contraceptive measures. When it is applied to leaders (as in the case of leaders of grassroots governments of Panchayats) these couples will then be considered models and other couples will follow their example. The success of using such a norm in local government institutions of Panchayats, that too through a law, assumes that law can make people decide to have small families.

It further assumes: (i) that people including the poor who tend to have many children, will aspire for leadership positions and hence follow the norm to fulfil their aspiration. The introduction of this norm in Panchayats almost simultaneously with the guaranteed entry of SC/ST and women across caste and class with reservations for them by the 73rd Constitutional Amendment shows a clear assumption of linking their consequent emerging political aspirations with legally prescribed conditionality of fertility choices; (ii) that local political leaders are seen as social models and, therefore, others will follow them in their desired family composition; (iii) that the choice of number of children is independent of the sex of the children; (iv) that health services are adequately available and affordable and accessible to give confidence for survival of children among all sections; and (v) that contraceptive services are universally available and equally accessible to all. It also assumes that these assumptions are equally applicable to women and men. Each of these assumptions is questionable especially when seen in the context of past experience of coercive measures and of the ground realities.

Many sociologists argue that these assumptions are not true and the application of any such norm has to take into consideration the ground realities. Son preference is a social reality in India as also seen in China and women may not be able to make binding decisions over the number of children they have and may not have equitable access to reproductive and child health services. Given these circumstances the two-child norm may have adverse implications that would tend to impinge on the rights, especially reproductive rights of men and women, and lead to discrimination against the girl child. When applied to the elected representatives or aspirants to elected positions in Panchayats it has serious implications for the democratic rights and participation especially of the weaker sections and women and youth seen against the intent and mandate of the 73rd Constitutional Amendment.

This monograph discusses the two-child norm currently being implemented in Panchayats and other sub-state-level elected bodies in some states, based on the results of our exploratory study conducted in Panchayats in the five states in the country. The study provided an exploratory examination in the concerned states on whether there is any basis for the assumptions stated above, and whether the application of the norm enforced through a law has the potential of negatively affecting the overall status of women and on the democratic participation of women, weaker sections and youths.

NOTES

1. Buch, Nirmala 1999, *From Oppression to Assertion: A Study of Women's Experience in Panchayats,* CWDS (Mimeo) Centre for Women's Development Studies, New Delhi.
2. Operationally five state studies on a uniform framework.
3. Balwant Rai Committee Report 1957, Ashok Mehta Committee Report, 1978.

2

The Study: Panchayats, Two-Child Norm, Population and Development

Recent Trends in Population Growth Rate in India

India joined China in the billionaires club in the year 2000 and the population growth rate continues to be high. This high growth rate often becomes a nightmare for the development planners conditioned as they are by the discourse of Population Bomb and Population Explosion. But before concluding that the large number of children in all families contribute to this high growth rate in India it may be worthwhile to consider certain ground realities in our country.

Population growth results from an excess of birth rates over death rates. In India since independence in 1947 there has been a rapid decline in the death rates, but this tremendous achievement has been offset by the not so rapid decline in the birth rates. Demographers say that this is natural. Among other changes, the life expectancy has increased to about 23 years, or more than one and a half times what it was (40 years) in the past 50 years. Women have less than half the children they had (TFR has reduced from 6 to 2.85) and use of contraceptives has increased around five times, but the population growth continues to be high because the country has a very young population and there are large numbers in their reproductive phase—the phenomenon of population momentum. There are a few other factors contributing to the high population growth rate which are substantially due to the inadequacies of health and family welfare services and social and cultural pressures.

These factors are:

- The high unmet needs for contraceptives among couples desiring smaller families,
- High levels of unwanted fertility in some places due to high infant mortality,
- Poor quality of care of health services, and
- Early age of marriage and early pregnancies and son preference.

The implications and consequences of the two-child norm have to be seen in the context of these factors as well. All these factors require that the state fulfils its obligation of providing quality care services and giving some hope for the survival of children, especially of those sections and in those areas on whom the externally imposed two-child norm seeks to place the responsibility for compliance of the norm. But the law places this duty completely on the individual citizens particularly women and seeks to enforce it by the penalty of their exclusion from the very political space guaranteed to them by the 73rd Constitutional Amendment after decades of their marginalisation.

Rationale for the Study

The 73rd Constitutional Amendment provided a new impetus to democracy by not only mandatorily extending it to the grassroots level throughout the country but also providing new spaces for women to participate through the provision of one-third reservation for women across castes/classes in all Panchayats. The National Population Policy 2000 provided a broad canvas for understanding and responding to population related concerns, placing people and sustainable development as central concerns. The concern for women's lower social status and for gender equality and women's empowerment is the common theme of the 73rd Constitutional Amendment and NPP 2000.

The provision of two-child norm for disqualifying persons having more than two children in contesting and holding Panchayat positions has been adopted by the concerned states in India with a view to reducing population growth rates and it is a matter of concern that it links population concerns with grassroots democracy just when it is being revived with a more inclusive composition of weaker sections, women and youth and with more clearly spelt out powers, resources and tenures. Hence the need to examine the practice, consequences and impact of this norm on the lives of people and in the context of the principles of the NPP.

Objectives and Scope

The objectives of the study were to:

(1) Understand the implications and consequences of the two-child norm in Panchayat laws on men and women with special reference to their ability to make reproductive choices, gender equality and democratic rights;
(2) Identify and document the legal and other constraints and effects of implementing the norm from the viewpoint of those affected directly or indirectly, legally or otherwise;
(3) Make recommendations based on the findings of the study.

The scope of the study included:

- A historical perspective of the evolution of the Panchayat system and the norm in the different states.
- The various procedures which are necessary to implement the provisions of the norm.
- The opinion of key respondents (unaffected persons) about the rationale, benefits and implications of the norm.
- Court rulings, if any, in the different states.
- The socio-economic profile of a sample of disqualified persons.
- The personal consequences of implementing the norm in the form of reactions and the response of those who had been affected.

- Examining issues of gender equality, reproductive choices and democratic rights.
- Emerging concerns.

Methodology

The study was exploratory and qualitative in nature and used a combination of secondary and primary data. We have explored through opinions and reactions of policy makers, programme implementers and civil society actors, how the norm was perceived and how it was being implemented at the state level. We investigated the experiences of those individuals who were affected by the norm. As a qualitative study it sought to look at the norm and its consequences primarily through the experiences of these affected persons. Affected individuals were seen as those who faced complaints or legal proceedings for disqualification for violating the norm or were prevented from contesting for this reason.

The design of the study was aimed at identifying what kind of cases/data exists and how can this information be constructively used in understanding the implications of the norm or re-examining it. The secondary data included records of legislative debates, data from State Election Commissions, district and sub-district level Panchayat Department offices, judicial rulings and media reports. The desk review included policy documents, government orders and the relevant Panchayat laws. Primary data were qualitative in nature and included semi-structured interviews, detailed case studies as well as Focus Group Discussions (FGDs) to cover both opinions and experiences. For functional reasons it consisted of five state-level studies. Each of the state-level studies followed a similar design and reporting protocol.

Five of the seven states, which adopted the two-child norm till the time of the study, were included in the study, thereby making it a fairly representative sample. The two exceptions were Himachal Pradesh where the application of law was from even a later date than Madhya Pradesh and Chhattisgarh (which inherited the law from Madhya Pradesh in November, 2000). Within the state a two-pronged approach was adopted. Where the historical perspective and broader implementation procedures were concerned the whole state was taken as one. Thus the desk review as well as primary level data up to key respondents were included for the whole state. However, where individual experiences of disqualification are concerned a couple of districts were selected in each state.

Initially, two districts had been selected for each state but later the choice of district was influenced by the availability of data. Thus three districts in Andhra Pradesh were included. In Orissa too the districts could not be chosen through any planned basis but on the availability of cases. In Rajasthan, Haryana and Madhya Pradesh a more informed choice of districts was possible but in Madhya Pradesh there were no cases of persons affected by this law either in the selected districts or elsewhere till the field work was almost over and then there was a sudden deluge of cases in places other than the selected districts from November, 2001. Hence additional districts were included to capture the experience of affected persons. Details of the districts are given in Table 2.1.

Table 2.1: States and districts in the study

States	*Districts*
Andhra Pradesh	Mahboob Nagar, Nalgonda, Ranga Reddy
Haryana	Ambala, Faridabad, Gurgaon
Madhya Pradesh	Betul, Bhopal, Hoshangabad, Neemuch, Sehore, Vidisha
Orissa	Angul, Cuttack, Dhenkanal, Khordha
Rajasthan	Ajmer, Alwar, Sawai Madhopur

The selection of respondents in the field study was purposive to include those concerned with the knowledge, experience or concern with the policies, programmes or effect of this law, issues of Panchayats, gender and health programmes. The respondents included:

- Panchayat persons affected by the norm: Interviews and case-studies.
- Panchayat persons not yet affected by the norm: Interviews.
- Persons in leadership, opinion makers or officials: Interviews.
- Community: Focus Group discussions.

Individuals, initially 20 in each state, were purposively chosen through a process of identification of individuals who had been affected by the norm either in contesting a Panchayat election or in holding Panchayat office later. In Madhya Pradesh these were chosen as additional cases when cases of disqualification for violation of the norm were suddenly started. The total number of the selected cases was not to represent a proportion of the number of cases in the concerned district but to explore the experiences and consequences of the norm on persons who experienced them. Forty individual case studies were prepared of a smaller number of the respondents to understand their life histories and the consequences of the norm in greater depth and detail.

The key respondents from the government side included a wide range of people from very high ranking policy-making officials like the Panchayat Minister (in one case) and the Principal Secretary, Panchayat and Rural Development (in one case), to programme implementers like Collectors, Deputy Collectors and Chief Medical Officers right down to the village-level functionaries like Anganwari workers of ICDS projects.

The key respondents from civil society included media persons, lawyers and NGO representatives. Care was taken to include lawyers who had experience or information of handling cases related to disqualification under the two-child norm. The NGO representatives were chosen from those NGOs which had some experience in working on women's issues or issues of social justice, or with Panchayats after the entry of a critical mass of women and weaker sections in the 1990s. Details of the different kinds of 262 respondents and 12 FGDs who were included in the study are outlined in Table 2.2.

Table 2.2: Respondents in the five states

State	*Respondents*	*Key Respondents*		*Community*
		Govt. Officials	*Others*	FGD
Andhra Pradesh	23	10	14	2
Haryana	22	08	14	2
Madhya Pradesh	20 + 18*	11	19	4**
Orissa	20 + 7*	16	11	2
Rajasthan	26	11	12	2
Total	111 + 25*	56	70	12

* The 25 respondents were those not yet affected by the norm.

** Additional FGDs in the second phase due to disqualification cases started in November 2001 only.

Fieldwork

The research teams at each state level included research associates and research investigators, and the team was coordinated by a project coordinator. Nearly all the members of the research teams held post-graduate degrees and had experience of fieldwork. Field-work took place in all five states between July 2001 and March 2002. In some places fieldwork took place in one phase, in others it was done in two phases. In Orissa disruption due to floods divided the fieldwork into three phases.

Limitations and Constraints

By virtue of being qualitative the study did not provide any ratings and percentages of the incidence and different impacts of the norm. It provided insights into human experiences and details about the nature and complexities of the experiences of the respondents, and the perspectives and opinions of the policy-makers, programme implementers and civil society.

The study faced the constraint of unavailability of state-level data of even the formally affected persons especially in the context of the time frame of short five state studies. The lack of reliable data at the state level in some states and in the case of Madhya Pradesh the sudden surge of disqualification cases when the field-work was almost over, forced us to include additional districts in the sample. In two states, where some data about the number of cases of persons affected by the law was available at the state level, it was not confirmed at the district and sub-district levels.

The implementation of the two-child norm was not uniform across the states in terms of the years of implementation, i.e. 1995, 1997 or 2001, and the availability of data about the number of violation of norm cases even formally instituted by the competent authorities. Besides, the expected impact on limiting the family size to two children to meet the conditionality of the law, effects of the law debarring persons exceeding the two-child norm are expected to be seen in persons not contesting election, their nominations for contest rejected on this ground or in their subsequent disqualification by competent authorities after being elected.

Information about persons disqualified at the time of filing of nominations to contest Panchayat election was not available anywhere. Regarding those who faced legal proceedings for disqualification after being elected, while Haryana and Rajasthan had some level of data at the state level, Andhra Pradesh and Orissa had none. In Andhra Pradesh, some officials said that there was apathy in following the norm. In Orissa there was a sense of reluctance among the officials to an external review of this law.

Evolution of Panchayat Structure and the Two-Child Norm in Panchayats

The institution of Village Panchayat is not new in India. Its historical evolution is from the traditional Village Panchayats which were based on social consensus. Village Panchayats were introduced as statutory institutions with the provincial Panchayat legislations in the colonial times. The Constitution of India included the Directive Principle of State Policy in Article 40 exhorting the states to organise Village Panchayats and to endow them with necessary powers to function as units of self-government. Later, committees[3] recommended a two- or three-tier Panchayat structure. State Panchayat laws were enacted accordingly and amended from time to time and the country had two- or three-tier Panchayat structure with Panchayats at village and district levels and at an intermediate level in different states. The Panchayats, however, had made an uneven progress in terms of their composition, powers and responsibilities, autonomy and continuity in different states. Their evolution and development was influenced by the perception that they were sharing in the political space occupied by representatives at the higher level.

The 73rd Constitutional Amendment made a new beginning by providing for mandatory elections every five years, a three-tier Panchayat structure from village to district, an inclusive composition with guaranteed representation to the weaker sections according to their population in the area and one-third representation to women across caste and class besides facilitating entry of youth through reducing the minimum age of entry to these institutions to 21 years.

The two-child norm clause was included in the state Panchayat laws enacted or amended to conform to the changes introduced by the 73rd Amendment. The two-child norm has no direct relation to the character and functions of these local government institutions. The norm, as formulated, directly and indirectly impacts entry and continuation of exactly those sections which were mandatorily included by the 73rd Amendment. When the norm was recommended by the NDC Committee on Population and was introduced by Rajasthan in its Panchayat and municipal laws in 1992, this new composition of Panchayats was very much under active consideration. It had already been proposed and gone up to Parliament as the 64th Amendment in 1988 and was then under active consideration as the 72nd Amendment Bill before the Joint Committee of Parliament. Hence, it is surprising that those who suggested this measure in the state Panchayat laws from the point of view of its perceived contribution to "population control" did not pause to consider its likely impact on women, weaker sections and youth who were sought to be included in the democratic grassroots institutions of Panchayats. In the excitement about the new initiative to revive Panchayats, this law did not receive adequate attention of various sections engaged in the discourse on Panchayats, development, gender and social justice. It may, however, be added that at least at the Central Government level the NDC Committee's recommendations did not get immediately accepted due to these reservations.

Rajasthan was the first state to introduce the two-child norm for Panchayats and municipalities in 1992 even before the NDC Committee made the recommendation about introducing it for political offices from Panchayats to Parliament. Of the five states under study Madhya Pradesh (undivided, before the creation of Chhattisgargh in November, 2000) was the last with the two-child norm being introduced eight years later in January, 2000. We look at the Panchayat structure and evolution of the two-child norm in Panchayats in the five states:

Andhra Pradesh

When Andhra Pradesh state was first constituted it inherited the Panchayat laws and structures of the areas, which were merged to form the state. After the formation of Andhra Pradesh the state enacted the Andhra Pradesh Gram Panchayats Act, 1964, repealing the Madras Village Panchayats Act, 1950 and the Hyderabad Village Panchayat Act, 1956. The Andhra Pradesh Panchayat Samitis and Zila Parishad Act, 1959 resulted in the setting up of a Panchayat Samiti for each block and a Zila Parishad for each district. Thus a three-tier system of Panchayat Raj emerged in the state. The state later introduced Mandals in place of Panchayat Samitis in blocks.

The Andhra Pradesh Panchayat Raj Act of 1994, enacted to conform to the provisions of the 73rd Constitutional Amendment introduced the two-child norm in the Zila Parishads, Mandal Parishads and Gram Panchayats. The two-child norm was applied to the Panchayat elections in June, 1995 and August, 2001.

Haryana

Haryana was formed in 1966 by bifurcating Punjab into Haryana and Punjab states. The new state of Haryana continued with the Punjab Gram Panchayat Act, 1952 and the Punjab Panchayat Samiti Act, 1961 with a three-tier Panchayat structure at the village, block and district level. The state government had set up an *ad hoc* committee in 1972 whose recommendation to abolish the Zila Parishads was accepted. In 1994 the state enacted the Haryana Panchayat Raj Act to conform to the requirements of the 73rd Amendment and restored the three-tier structure as mandated by this Amendment. This incorporated the two-child norm. Although introduced in 1994, the norm was made applicable from 1995. Since then the state has had two Panchayat elections, one prior to the cut-off date of operationalisation of the two-child norm in 1995 and the second in 2000.

Madhya Pradesh

The state of Madhya Pradesh came into existence on 1 November, 1956 as a result of the reorganisation of states on a linguistic basis. The state was bifurcated into the present Madhya Pradesh and Chhattisgarh on 1 November, 2000. The state inherited the Panchayat laws and structure of its constituting states in 1956. Successive new Panchayat laws were introduced in 1962, 1980 and 1990. The present structure is governed by the Madhya Pradesh Panchayat Raj Act, 1993 enacted to conform to the 73rd Amendment. Since then two general elections to Panchayats have been held in 1994 and early 2000. Madhya Pradesh is one of the latest states to have included two-child norm in their Panchayat legislation through a special amendment. It has also extended the norm to include elections to municipalities, agricultural produce marketing committees *(mandis)* and cooperatives. The state has also applied the norm for the denial of state programme benefits e.g. loans, subsidy, poverty alleviation programmes and entry in government jobs to those who exceed the norm—a policy being adopted by a number of other states also.

It was immediately after holding the municipal and Panchayat elections in early 2000 that the state cabinet decided to introduce the two-child norm which was then adopted by the legislature by a single-line amendment on 29 March, 2000 debarring a person who has more than two living children one of whom is born on or after 26 January, 2001 for election to Panchayats. The amendment was notified only on 31 May, 2000. This became a contested issue when a person who had an additional child in January, 2001, questioned how he could have been disqualified for the birth of a child within eight months of the new law.

Orissa

In Orissa, the Panchayat structure and its functioning is governed by three pieces of legislation—Gram Panchayat Act 1965, Panchayat Samiti Act 1959 and Zila Parishad Act 1991—as opposed to other states in our study where there is only one

Panchayat Act. Similar provisions were introduced in all the three Acts when the state decided to introduce the two-child norm. The two-child norm was made applicable to the Zila Parishads in November, 1993 and in the Gram Panchayats and Panchayat Samitis simultaneously in April, 1994.

When the words "Has more than two children" were added as a disqualification with prospective effect, two other grounds for disqualification were also introduced, namely, literacy (if a person *is not able to read and write Oriya)* and bigamy (*has more than one spouse living*). However, the illiteracy criterion was applied only to the block and district level, thereby allowing more women and men irrespective of their level of literacy to contest at the village level. The norm became applicable in the Panchayat Elections of 1997 held under the amended law.

Rajasthan

The first Panchayat Act of Rajasthan was enacted in 1953. The Rajasthan Panchayat Samiti and Zila Parishad Act came in 1959. The state then had a three-tier Panchayat structure with a Gram Panchayat for a village or group of villages, a Panchayat Samiti for a block and a Zila Parishad for a district. All the states were obliged to bring their Panchayat laws in conformity with the 73rd Amendment within one year expiring in April 1994. Hence, the Rajasthan Panchayat Raj Act, 1994 was also enacted and came into effect from 23 April, 1994. With this law Rajasthan continued with a three-tier system of Panchayat Raj.

The two-child norm was introduced in 1992, through an ordinance which stipulated that one year after its coming into effect, a person who had an additional child (more than two or more living children) would be disqualified for being a Panchayat representative. But no elections were held under this amended law. The clause was then included in the 1994 Panchayat Raj Act and the violation of the two-child norm became one of the 13 grounds for disqualification, but without the one-year grace period. Hence, anyone having an additional child (besides two or more living children) after April, 1994 would have been ineligible for contesting Panchayat elections. A similar law was also passed for the municipal bodies in the state. Two changes had to be made in it on popular pressure. The one year's grace period was virtually restored by postponing the date for effect of this clause to one year after election and the first post-73rd Amendment Panchayat elections were held without applying this norm.

Implementing the Two-Child Norm

In all states there is a cut-off date beyond which the birth of a third child or more children constitutes a violation. This effectively means that the norm is applicable only to those persons who are in the active reproductive age group, and exempts older individuals who have completed their families. Also when the norm is legislated, the cut-off date is often a year later in the future whereby it gives an advance notice to intending parents that their reproductive decisions may affect their democratic liberties/ambitions.

Andhra Pradesh

The two-child restriction is one of the 12 grounds of disqualification. The disqualification is operative only after the decision of the competent authority. In the case of the Gram Panchayat the competent authority is the munsif magistrate. In the case of Mandal and Zila representatives an individual member can also request clarification from the competent authority. It is important to note that no procedure for disqualification can be initiated without a complaint.

Haryana

The powers to disqualify sitting members of Gram Panchayats are with the Deputy Commissioner of the district. Thereafter the disqualified individuals can file appeals before the Financial Commissioner (Revenue and Panchayats) and may also resort to judicial remedy. If the disqualification is upheld, the vacancy is reported to the State Election Commission for holding bye-elections. The Director, Panchayats, or the Deputy Commissioners concerned can suspend or remove a Sarpanch or Panch after making an inquiry and after giving a show-cause notice. There is a similar provision for the government to take action against a member, Pradhan, Up-Pradhan of Panchayat Samiti or member of the Zila Parishad.

Madhya Pradesh

The new Panchayat Act passed in 1993 had 12 grounds for disqualification to which the government added, in 2000, a 13th ground, of the birth of a third or additional child. The process of disqualification of a Panchayat representative for violation of the two-child norm starts with the filing of an application or by the competent authority taking it up on her/his own. This is followed by a hearing. The competent authority for Gram and Janpad Panchayats is the District Collector while the Divisional Commissioner is the competent authority for the Zila Panchayat. The aggrieved person can file an appeal to the Commissioner (in the case of Gram and Janpad Panchayats) or the Board of Revenue (in the case of a Zila Panchayat) and the decision on appeal is final.

Orissa

While the two-child norm was introduced in 1993, it was effectively implemented only after the Panchayat Election in 1997. The Collector of a district is the competent authority to decide on disqualification of Gram Panchayat representatives. The District Judge is the competent authority for the other levels. Where the District Collector is the competent authority she/he can act on the complaint of others as well as take *suo motu* (self initiated) action. The Collector has to make an enquiry, hear out the person concerned and then pass an order which is final and conclusive. In the case of a Panchayat Samiti or a Zila Parishad the complaint has to be made by the member concerned or another member. If the samiti or parishad decides to raise the issue it is mandatory for its Chairperson or President to make the complaint to the District Judge.

Rajasthan

While Rajasthan was the first to introduce the two-child norm it actually put it into practice three years later after elections to Panchayats were held in 1995. This disqualification clause was applied with prospective effect (after the election) to the elected representatives violating the norm. When a Panchayat member faces disqualification (including the violation of the two-child norm), the competent authority declares that a person has become ineligible. Initially, the District Judge decided the question of disqualification and the office of a chairperson and deputy chairperson became vacant if the holder of the office was disqualified (Sections 40 and 41). The Act was later amended so that the competent executive authority can finally decide about disqualification of an elected representative without judicial adjudication.The Divisional Commissioner is the competent authority in the case of Gram Panchayat representatives while the state government decides in the case of Panchayat Samiti and Zila Parishad representatives. These officials have to act only on complaints about a person having violated the norm. They do not have the power to initiate action on their own

Population and Development: Background of the Five States

We have tried to understand why the particular states opted to introduce this clause and if there were strong reasons for its introduction. We have also tried to see what the gender related indicators indicate in these states. We noted that the five states which formed the basis of our study are not only from different parts of the country (Haryana—North, AP—South, Orissa—East, Rajasthan—West and MP—Central) but also have different social and economic characteristics. Tables 2.3, 2.4, 2.5 summarise some of the key population, development and gender-related indicators for the five states. The data for these tables have been obtained from the Census 2001, two National Family Health Surveys and National Human Development Report 2001.

The key indicators of decadal population growth rate, total fertility rate (TFR), unmet contraceptive needs, contraceptive use, changes in couple protection rate, sex ratio, child sex ratio and decadal change in it and male-female literacy gap in the five states give a varied picture. Table 2.3 compares population related indicators for India and the five study states. Two states, AP and Orissa, have decadal growth rates significantly lower than the country as a whole. The total fertility rate in these two states is also lower than the national average while in Haryana it is roughly the same as the national average. Contraceptive prevalence is also much higher in AP and Haryana than the national average and the unmet needs less than half the national average. If one looks at the percentage growth in contraceptive prevalence between the two rounds of the National Family Health Survey, all five states have much higher changes in the contraceptive prevalence than at the national level. These, therefore, do not justify the anxiety shown at the introduction of this coercive measure in these states.

Table 2.3: Population related indicators

States	*Decadal growth rate %*	*TFR*	*Unmet need %*	*Contrace-ptive Use %*	*Change in CPR in NFHS II %*
Andhra Pradesh	13.86	2.25	7.7	59.6	27
Haryana	28.06	2.88	7.6	62.4	26
Madhya Pradesh	24.34	3.31	16.2	44.3	21
Orissa	15.94	2.46	15.5	46.8	29
Rajasthan	28.33	3.78	17.6	40.3	27
India	21.34	2.85	15.8	48.2	19

Table 2.4 compares the gender-related indicators in these states. In Rajasthan and Madhya Pradesh the literacy gap between the sexes is much higher than the national average, while Haryana has reported an alarming decline in the juvenile sex ratio. All the five states have a declining juvenile sex ratio. These indicate a need of serious concern about the implications of the coercive

two-child norm particularly in the grassroots-level institutions in these states.

Table 2.4: Gender related indicators

States	*M-F literacy gap*	*Sex ratio*	*Under 6 sex ratio*	*Decadal change in child sex ratio*
Andhra Pradesh	39%	978	964	–11
Haryana	41%	861	820	–59
Madhya Pradesh	51%	920	929	–12
Orissa	49%	972	950	–17
Rajasthan	72%	922	909	–7
India	41%	933	927	–18

Table 2.5 compares some overall development indicators, namely, the Net State Domestic Product (1997-98), the percentage

Table 2.5: Overall development indicators

States	*NSDP*	*% below BPL*	*HDI rank*
Andhra Pradesh	2550	15.77	10/15
Haryana	4025	8.74	5/15
Madhya Pradesh	1922	37.43	12/15
Orissa	1666	47.15	11/15
Rajasthan	2226	15.28	9/15
India	2840	26.10	–

of the population below the poverty line (1999-2000) and the Human Development Index rank (2001). Haryana is clearly the front runner among these states on all three counts. All the other states have a significantly lower Net State Domestic Product. While AP, Haryana and Rajasthan have some degree of economic parity, Madhya Pradesh and Orissa have more than a third and almost a full half of their population living under the poverty line.

3

Experiences and Perspectives of Panchayat Representatives

Panchayat Representatives affected by the Two-Child Norm

One of the serious difficulties faced in conducting the study was lack of data about the persons affected by this (two-child) law. Since the provision was included as part of a policy to motivate individuals particularly Panchayat leaders to adopt the small family norm, it was reasonable to expect monitoring of disqualification of panchayat leaders on this ground and of what was happening to the Panchayats as a result of this law. We found that despite the fact that disqualifications are subject of judicial/quasi-judicial cases, in most of the states no data were being kept/collected about the number and details of cases.

Where data were available from various sources, they showed a large number of disqualifications for violation of the two-child norm. In Rajasthan between 1995 and 1997, 412 cases of disqualification had been documented. One study in Rajasthan had estimated 1,579 disqualifications. The latest round of Panchayat elections in Rajasthan was in January and February, 2000. According to the legal cell of the Panchayat Raj Department, as on mid-November, 2001, there were 3,000 court cases relating to disqualification on all counts, e.g. misuse of power, misconduct, financial irregularity, violation of two-child norm, etc. Of these, violation of the two-child norm accounted for roughly 10 per cent of the total cases.

In Andhra Pradesh and Orissa very little data were available at any level. It was difficult to obtain information in Orissa regarding disqualification for violating the two-child norm from a centralised source. The Orissa State Election Commission gave a list of seven cases in nine districts. However, a quick visit to 10 districts showed 27 cases in 9 districts. There are admittedly a large number of disqualifications for which data are available only in individual case files. For instance, one of the districts which gave details of cases which formed part of these 27 cases reported that about 20 cases existed there but that these would be inaccessible, even at that level. Data were similarly not available in Andhra Pradesh. Most cases here were pending in civil courts with stay orders on the disqualification notices. These indicate a clear trend of a large number of disqualifications being only for violating the two child-norm.

In Haryana it was difficult to obtain information/records at the state level. The petitioners approach different appellate authorities, e.g. Financial Commissioner (Revenue and Panchayats), High Court and even Supreme Court after decisions in the original case. The vacant positions are reported to the State Election Commission for holding bye-elections. But these do not reflect the number of complaints and proceedings completed but still subject to appeals and stay orders. Further, no data were available about the situation prior to the second Panchayat general elections of 2000. Table 3.1 shows the number of persons disqualified on various grounds including violation of the two-child norm in a period of 16 months. A large proportion of the

Table 3.1: Panchayat members disqualified in Haryana from March, 2000 to June, 2001

Level		*Men*	*Women*	*Total**
Zila Parishad		1	1	2(2)
Panchayat Samiti		8	6	14 (12)
Gram Panchayat	Sarpanch	74	27	101(31)
	Panch	200	70	270(230)
Total		283	104	387(275)

Source: State Election Commission, Haryana.

* Figures in brackets show the number of persons disqualified for violating the two-child norm.

disqualifications are for violating the two-child norm and in all the cases except those against the Sarpanches it is the overwhelming reason. The actual number for the state as a whole will be larger as we noted during our field work that 166 cases were instituted for violation of the two-child norm in only three study districts in this period.

In Madhya Pradesh, the law became effective from 26 January, 2001 but there was no awareness of the law and no legal proceedings had been started under this law till November, 2001, i.e. for almost one year. Some of the senior state government officers as well as the elected representatives and media persons were convinced that the legal norm would come into effect only at the time of the next Panchayat general election in 2005. The first phase of the field work for our study in August, 2001 showed that a number of elected representatives in many Panchayats had violated the norm, but neither they knew about the norm nor was any action started by the members of the community or by those having the responsibility for enforcing the norm. This was despite the provision in this state law that the Collector/Commissioner could start proceedings himself without waiting for complaints.

In November, 2001 the news of the disqualification notice to a woman Gram Panchayat Sarpanch in Neemuch district, which borders the district of Chittorgarh in Rajasthan, was published. Thereafter there was a spate of complaints and disqualifications across the state. By the end of March, 2002, the number of complaints/cases as reported in the media rose to 52 in the seven districts of Neemuch, Sagar, Guna, Chhindwara, Sehore, Hoshangabad and Chhatarpur. There were many other cases which did not find mention in the media. In Panna, there were already 57 complaints of violation of the two-child norm in the district and 164 Panchayat members had been served notices for violating this norm.

Information collected by the study team in Rajasthan showed that in a period of about one and a half years after the elections in 2000, 63 persons (53 men and 10 women) had been finally disqualified for violating the two-child norm. They included one member each of Zila Parishad and Panchayat Samiti. The others were Panches and Sarpanches of Gram Panchayats, with the number of Sarpanches being disproportionately higher compared to the actual ratio between the Panch and Sarpanch in position. The court cases very often continued for prolonged periods.

Data collected by us later in 2004 has shown that in Haryana after the year 2000 when the last Panchayat election was held there were 1,552 disqualifications up to March, 2004. Of these, 1,350 (87 per cent) were for violation of the two-child norm and included 1,044 Panches, 249 Sarpanches, 49 members of Panchayat Samiti and 8 members of Zila Panchayat. Only 202 (13 per cent) cases were on other grounds for disqualification under the state law. Similarly, in Rajasthan after the election in 2000 total disqualifications up to March, 2004 were 808. Of them 508 (63%) were for violation of the two-child norm and 300 (37%) were on other grounds.

In MP there were 2,122 disqualifications. Of these 1,140 (54%) disqualifications for the violation of the two-child norm and 982 (46%) were on other grounds. There were reports of a large number of such cases pending in the districts after the issue of notices and replies and these could be decided any time. Chhattisgarh which had inherited this law from MP had disqualification of 766 persons for violation of the two-child norm. These included 143 Sarpanches and 623 Panches and 228 cases were pending for decision. Only 357 disqualifications were on other grounds. So in a total of 1,123, the two-child norm disqualification cases were 68 per cent. While in these states we could thus have these data to make an assessment, Andhra Pradesh and Orissa could give no data even in 2004. In fact one response indicated only two cases in AP and three cases in Orissa in this period which could not be accepted without further field checks in view of our past experience during the study. Data collected in 2004 after the study was completed are given in Table 3.2.

Among those who were removed in MP, 72 per cent belonged to the scheduled castes, scheduled tribes and other backward classes. In Chhattisgarh of those disqualified for violation of the two-child norm, data which could be available for 9 out of the16 districts showed 20 per cent SC and 17 per cent ST among those so disqualified.

Table 3.2: Panchayat representatives disqualified for violation of the two-child norm after the 2000 election till 2004

State	*Panch*	*Sarpanch*	*Member*		*Total*
			Panchayat Samiti	*Zila Panchayat*	
Haryana	1044	249	49	08	1350
Madhya Pradesh	857	270	11	02	1140
Chhattisgarh	623	143	–	–	766
Rajasthan	390	96	17	05	508
Andhra Pradesh	–	–	–	–	No data
Orissa	–	–	–	–	No data
Total	2914	758	77	15	3764

Note: Elections in AP in 2001, and in Orissa in 2002.

Figures in Table 3.2 do not show the number of those who are not able to follow the norm and, therefore, (i) do not seek to contest election or (ii) whose nominations have been rejected and also (iii) those who have violated the norm and are in constant tension as they can face such proceedings if anyone complains or an enthusiastic official starts proceedings against them with a view to making his contribution to the goal of "population control". We found instances in districts where suddenly certain officials took such an initiative and immediately cases in hundreds were started for issue of notices and disqualifying Panchayat representatives. Similarly, there were persons who had violated the norm but no complaints were made and so no proceedings had started to disqualify them. This was seen even in the Panchayats where one or more representatives had been disqualified and removed. The reasons for not complaining related to lack of interest in action against them or fear and pressure of the powerful person violating the norm.

Experiences of Panchayat Representatives facing Disqualification

Socio-economic Background

A total of 136 Panchayat representatives were respondents in this study. Of them 111 were those facing disqualifications. Twenty-five were those who had not faced it so far but were interviewed to get their perspectives, as implementation had not started in MP when we completed the first phase of the fieldwork and in Orissa where the data were not available about such persons till they were located through informal channels. All of them were interviewed and 40 case studies were prepared. The socio-economic background of 111 Panchayat representatives (respondents) facing disqualification is provided in Table 3.3.

Table 3.3: Socio-economic background of the respondents facing disqualification

State	*Age*		*Sex*		*Caste*				*Income (pa)*	
	21-49	*50*	*M*	*F*	*SC*	*ST*	*OBC*	*Gen*	*<20K*	*>20K*
A.P.	23	–	12	11	7	1	15	–	9	14
Haryana	21	1	14	8	6	–	4	12	8	14
M.P.	19	1	13	7	9	3	6	2	14	6
Orissa	19	1	8	12	10	1	7	2	18	2
Rajasthan	24	2	19	7	8	–	12	6	4	22
Total	106	5	66	45	40	5	44	22	53	58

The following picture emerges from Table 3.3:

- Women form 41 per cent of the respondents while the overall proportion of women in Panchayats is a little over a third of the membership.
- Scheduled castes, tribes and backward castes form an overwhelming 80 per cent of the respondents.
- Roughly 50 per cent have an annual income of less than 20,000 rupees.
- Most representatives were in the age bracket 21 to 49 years.

Table 3.4: Posts held by Panchayat representatives affected by the two-child norm

Panchayat Representative	*Andhra Pradesh*	*Haryana*	*Madhya Pradesh*	*Orissa*	*Rajasthan*	Total
Panch	08	13	4+2	9	18	54
Sarpanch	14	08	14	11	07	54
Member PS	01	01	–	–	–	02
President PS	–	–	–	–	01	01
Member ZP	–	–	–	–	–	–
President ZP	–	–	–	–	–	–
Total	23	22	20	20	26	111

As Table 3.4 shows, while there are 54 Panches affected, the number of Sarpanches were also equal while the proportion of Sarpanches in the Panchayat composition is generally one out of 10 or 15. Thus the Sarpanches who have an important leadership role in Panchayats are targeted for proceedings against them using this law. An overwhelmingly large number (95 per cent) of the representatives were from the village level. Overall the representatives facing disqualification were young (21–49 years), poor, predominantly from the scheduled castes and backward castes and a higher representation of women than the overall proportion of women representatives in Panchayats.

Contraceptive Use and Family Planning

The introduction of the two-child norm in Panchayats was expected to promote contraception so that more couples have smaller families. It was expected that those who faced proceedings for violation of this law had failed due to lack of knowledge, acceptance of the desirability of a small family or non-adoption of contraceptives. However, we found that most (80 per cent) of the affected representatives were aware of the importance of small families, and a little over a half (53 per cent) had adopted permanent methods but they did so after their desired family size and sex composition was completed.

Roughly a fourth (23 per cent) of the respondents were practising some form of contraception. But the disturbing factor was that we found at least 11 cases in which abortion had been induced and in four cases pre-natal sex determination had been done resulting in abortions in cases of female foetus report and continuation of pregnancy if the foetus was reported to be male.

There were differences among the states. Of the 23 Panchayat representatives interviewed in AP, the majority of those disqualified (15 out of 17) claimed to have adopted permanent means but only after they had obtained their desired family size. Most of the respondents were aware both of family planning methods and of the advantages of a small family. Their decision to go in for sterilization, they claimed, had no connection with their opting to contest the election. On the other hand, in the sample of 20 affected Panchayat representatives in Madhya Pradesh, only 12 were aware of family planning methods. Among them eight were practising some form of contraception. During the course of the study it was found that the elected representatives had tried to show a reduced number of children in their families so that it could be claimed that the norm had been followed.

There were cases where the respondents had resorted to desertion of their wives. The chief of a vernacular daily newspaper in AP mentioned that there had been cases at the Mandal level where some of the Panchayat representatives had divorced their wives on record to save their seats, but were also living together as husband and wife. But there were others who went ahead and had more children despite the two-child norm because of their own reasons.

Complaints, Disqualification and Circumvention of the Law

There were instances when cases of violation duly supported by appropriate documents went unheard. For instance, Ramlal (name changed) who had contested against Mukesh (name changed) for the post of Sarpanch in Sawai Madhopur district of Rajasthan had raised the issue of Mukesh's four children. Ramlal had filed an election petition with supporting documents including Anganwari record, birth-death register, immunisation record and ration card but reportedly no action had been taken against Mukesh and he won the election. In another case the 'Pramukh' as well as the members of the Zila Parishad knew about the violation of the norm by a Zila Parishad member from the Mina caste, but they were afraid to speak out because he came from a dominant tribe and belonged to the party in power. It was reported that those who had money or influence also succeeded in delaying or influencing an inquiry and prolonging the court proceedings so that they could continue in their posts despite violating the norm.

In Orissa the study revealed that ignorance of the norm was one of the main reasons for which the elected members faced disqualification. In fact, only 2 out of 20 representatives, who were interviewed here, said that they knew about the two-child norm prior to contesting the Panchayat elections. One person learnt it at the time of filing his nomination papers while 11 persons learnt about it when notices were served on them and six were unaware of the norm. As the action in any case of violation of the norm could be taken after complaints there were cases of the two-child norm being used to settle political scores.

Among the case studies in Andhra Pradesh there were three cases where the complaints were politically motivated. In two cases these representatives had held office earlier and the norm had been violated in their earlier term without any complaint having been made. In the third case the complaint was false because the third child was born before the cut-off date. All three cases were from the backward castes, and two of them were women. Interestingly in all three cases the couple had adopted the permanent method of contraception, before the election in which their disqualification was sought.

In Haryana the study team came across disqualified representatives who were certain that the complaints against them were politically motivated. They felt certain because there were other Panchayat members who had violated the norm but no complaints had been made against them. There were also disqualified representatives who contested the elections because they did not know of the norm. They claimed that they would not have contested had they known about the law. Haryana has a long history of Panchayat representatives approaching appellate courts in cases of complaints and show-cause notices. Some of the representatives in the study had also taken this route including the cases in the Javed and others *vs* State of Haryana and others decided by the Supreme Court in 2003.

Representatives who faced complaints with regard to the violation of the norm have used many strategies to deny the birth of a child or have hidden and misreported children or even tampered with or provided contrary documents. In Rajasthan the study team noted a variety of methods that had been used, sometimes successfully, sometimes not. In one case the child's horoscope, details in the ration-card and school records were provided as proof, but even then it didn't work. In another case the ANM's records had been tampered. In a third case the doctors certified that the child was not of the concerned representative and in a fourth the woman representative tried to hide her child among the other children in her joint family. In one case the OBC Sarpanch went for a sex-determination test and then went for an induced abortion to avoid disqualification.

In Haryana the study team came across different strategies to avoid disqualification. The common practice in Gurgaon district (in contrast to Ambala district) was to obtain stay orders from a higher authority. There were also five instances where the disputed children had been given in adoption to near relatives and adoption deeds obtained in some cases.

From the evidence available from interviews with representatives and from key informants it was seen that the different methods adopted to provide evidence in Andhra Pradesh were producing certificates – birth certificates as well as sterilization certificates, including certificates of failed sterilization. There were also cases of desertion of wives in this state.

In Orissa the desire to contest a complaint was less as the people were poorer and could not afford prolonged litigation. However, there were cases where the representative provided documents to prove that the complaint was ill founded.

In Madhya Pradesh those disqualified or facing disqualification used several tactics to avoid proceedings ranging from expressing ignorance about the norm to pushing the date(s) of their/spouse conception prior to the cut-off date. For this, they used Anganwari/ANM records and ration-cards. Some had given their children in adoption to relatives. In one case the couple planned to divorce each other to avoid disqualification.

Perspectives and Opinions

Government Officials

The opinions of government officials on the two-child norm in the five states can be broadly divided into the opinion of policy-makers and senior government officials at the state level and the opinion of implementers of the norm primarily officials at the district and sub-district level. As far as the senior government functionaries are concerned there is unanimity across the states about the importance of this provision in view of the "population problem" and "national interest". One senior health policy maker said, "How long can we wait for social development. Population problem is too serious." Another policy-maker concerned with Panchayats said, "Population is too serious a national problem. Everything is fair to deal with it."

Across the five states there was uniform acceptance of the assumption that this law would set an example for the leaders to adopt smaller families and this would then be adopted by the community at large. When asked about the potential of this law in increasing women's vulnerability to abortion or desertion the officials discounted the possibility. There was also a misplaced belief that an Indian woman elected to a Panchayat becomes so empowered that she could freely decide the timing and number of children irrespective of her family and spouse wanting differently and also that she will be able to resist social pressures for producing sons. At the implementation level this law was just one more condition which had to be met for eligibility or for disqualification. In most cases this condition was considered on a par with the other 11 or 12 conditions in the law.

However, there are a couple of opinions which are noteworthy. One official in Haryana noted that this provision was an important tool for harassment and called it the Harassment Act. In Orissa professors at a medical college called for harsher laws similar to the one-child norm in China, which is interesting in the light of the low population growth rate in Orissa. In Andhra Pradesh, which is the only southern state where this provision exists, a district medical officer claimed that this law was unnecessary considering the already near universal desire for small families.

Lawyers

The opinion of lawyers can be broadly divided into the opinion of those who practiced in High Courts and those who practice in subordinate courts. Across the five states there was agreement among the lawyers of the higher courts that the norm was justified. In the north Indian states the issue of national interest was also mentioned more than once. In Rajasthan there were more than one case with the High Court ruling in favour of the norm immediately after it came into force and lawyers agreed with the decision.

In one case a lawyer practising in a subordinate court in Andhra Pradesh was categorical that, "This act is deceiving the poor. The educated are deceiving the illiterate. Wrong certificates are being produced. Some people say they have given their child for adoption, others deny that the child is theirs ... all sorts of things happen. And, anyway, most candidates complete their term by the time the court trials are finalised ...". He was indicating the expenses the poor had to meet to contest the complaints, the malpractices followed to circumvent the law and the use of the stay orders from the courts to prolong the proceedings till the five-year period of an elected post is almost complete.

One lawyer in Orissa felt that the law violated the civil rights and was an invasion of privacy. In the case of lawyers who had handled such cases it was just another case and most felt that the problems in the implementation of the Act could be avoided with better dissemination of information about the Act.

Media

The role of the media in all the states had been limited to mentioning the fact that the Act existed and that there were cases of complaints and disqualification. Media persons across the five states mentioned that there had been little debate in the media about the norm vis-a-vis the democratic rights of the people especially women. There was also a feeling that this norm had made a modest beginning with the lower rungs of representatives and should be extended to cover the state level and national legislators as well.

NGO Leaders

Opinion among the members of the NGO community was mixed and this extended to all the states. While some supported the legislation, others felt that it was not in the interests of women and had a great potential for abuse. In some cases the NGO leaders felt that the norm affected Dalits and the poor adversely as well, because they tended to have larger families for various reasons. There were also instances where the NGOs admitted that they had not thought about the implications of this provision in the Panchayat Act though they had been engaged in the training and capacity building of Panchayat representatives.

Community Members

There was a difference of opinion regarding the two-child norm among members of the same community (those affected as well as those randomly selected from the community for focus group discussions). In places the men or the more well-off agreed that the norm was useful, whereas women and the poor did not agree. Members of the community also mentioned instances of use and misuse of this provision to settle scores. Mention was also made of the ways in which the norm was being circumvented by those who had resources. They had an additional or third child after the cut-off date but either no one complained or they were able to manage the inquiry proceedings or the court procedures. This was also confirmed by the case study experiences.

Focus group discussions with community members revealed that while the affluent may go unchallenged for violating the two-child norm and may afford to contest any litigation if they did get implicated, the poor, particularly women, were in no position to do so. Our case studies substantiated these observations. Thus while the complaint against an influential woman Sarpanch was closed because the female infant died (obviously of illness and neglect) another person who had a stillborn child was disqualified because, as the Commissioner, who decided the case, observed, he had done everything to violate the norm, it was only the nature which intervened to result in a stillbirth.

Legal and Judicial Perspectives

To the legal mind, the two-child norm is firmly positioned against issues such as population explosion, resource depletion and sustainable development, requiring measures to contain population growth. The norm, therefore, is not seen as directly interfering with the right of any citizen to take a decision in the matter of procreation. It is seen as only generating a legal consequence for a person who has had more than two children on the relevant date of seeking the elective office under the Act.

The courts have accepted the legality of this clause and rejected the arguments of violation of human rights, democratic rights, personal law of minorities or equality as the clause is not applicable to MPs/MLAs. The judgments have statements of concern about "Population Bomb", "Population Explosion". Apparently the efficacy of social development and women's empowerment to further the goal of population stabilisation on the one hand, and the likely negative consequences of law of two-child norm on the other hand, had not been brought up before the courts.

The Andhra Pradesh High Court upheld the validity of these provisions. Upholding the validity of sub-section 19(3) of the state law, the court observed, "The said provision has been incorporated in view of *the population explosion which is beyond imagination* .... There will be no place to live in and if there is a place to live in, there will be no place for other resources like agricultural land, water resources and other material resources for sustenance. If the population is not contained, leave apart food, we may not get potable water to drink. As such, *the restriction of the number of children for the elected representatives has got nexus with the object to be achieved, i.e. containing the population by the measure of practising family planning.* As such, there is no violation of any of the Constitutional rights and the provision is *intra vires* the Constitution". [Are Gangadhar *vs.* Zila Parishad, Karimnagar and others, 1995 (5) ALD 585 (DB): 1995 (5)] (emphasis added).

Similarly, in another case, the High Court observed that Section 19(3) does not directly interfere with the right of any citizen to take a decision in the matter of procreation. It only creates a legal disability on the part of any person who has procreated more than two children as on the relevant date of seeking an elected office under the Act. [B.K. Parathasarathi *vs.* Government of Andhra Pradesh and others, 2000(1) ALD 199(DB)].

The Punjab and Haryana High Court observed (in Fazru *vs.* State of Haryana and Lalaram *vs.* State of Haryana) in 1994, "to make life meaningful, worth living, the legislature can provide limiting one's family. *How can the State assure one the right to work, education and to public assistance in cases of unemployment, old age, sickness and disablement and in other cases of undeserved want, if there is no check on the growth of population?* Constitutional dream inhering in Article 41 of the Constitution of India will remain only an idle dream and will never be translated into reality if there is no check on population growth through some legislative measure". (emphasis added)

"It is observed that the government is spending a huge amount of money on propagating Family Planning. In the recent years, *the growth of population in the country is alarming. It is expected from the Panches and Sarpanches to set good examples* and they are supposed to maintain the norm of two children. *If they themselves violate the same, what examples they can set before the public.* The population can be checked by adopting the Family Planning measures. *If the same are not adopted, then the Nature takes its own turn, i.e. people die by natural calamities. Right to contest election is not a fundamental right.* We are not oblivious of the fact that the *nation's interest is supreme."*

"Growing population is the greatest problem, absolutely

essential for every country to see that the Family Planning Programme is maintained at a sufficient level so as *to meet the danger of over-population which, if not controlled, may lead to serious social and economic problems* throughout the country. No enactment, which promotes social and economic justice, can be held to be *ultra vires.* No doubt every citizen has a right to live with human dignity. But, *how can one expect citizens of this country to live with human dignity and social equality when the population goes on increasing by leaps and bounds. If the existing rate of growth of population is allowed to continue it is bound to take the country to a dangerous stage where persons may die of hunger and may not have a roof over their heads to live."* [1998 (1) PL 5] (emphasis added)

"The purpose of enacting this provision under challenge and the right to life, keeping in view the same, *cannot be extended in the manner that endless millions keep multiplying when everyone has thereafter to live an animal existence.* The restriction, therefore, cannot be termed to be arbitrary." (emphasis added)

The Rajasthan High Court considered the validity of this norm (Mukesh Kumar Ajmera and others *vs.* State of Rajasthan and others: AIR 1997 Rajasthan 250) and ruled that this provision "cannot be declared as arbitrary or discriminatory as no provision has been made with respect to the Members of Parliament, Members of State Legislative Assembly or the members of Cooperative Societies", etc. *"Though having more than two children does not, in any way, affect the working of the Sarpanch, Panch or a Member of a Panchayat Raj institution* but the population explosion has affected the economic condition of the state and it is with the purpose to implement the mandate of the Directive Principles of State Policy that this measure was considered necessary." (emphasis added)

As a result of these early judicial pronouncements, the Panchayat representatives have only tried to circumvent the law by adopting practices to show reduced number of children. It has also, to some extent, led to the issues and implications not being debated very widely. The negative consequences and ineffectiveness of coercive measures, the ICPD consensus, the spirit of the National Population Policy 2000 have not been adequately placed before the courts. Hence the courts could not look at social justice friendly and gender just, and hence more effective, route to achieve population stabilisation.

The Supreme Court's judgement in Javed and others *vs.* State of Haryana and others in July 2003 [2003(8) SCC] also appears to continue the same concern for "Population Control". The court accepted the constitutional validity of the Haryana law disqualifying persons with more than two living children to contest election to or continue in Panchayats, also observing that it seeks to achieve the objectives of popularising Family Welfare/Family Planning Programme. The submission that a person's number of children did not affect his capacity, competence and ability to serve the Panchayat office and had no nexus with the purpose of the Act was not accepted observing that since one of the objects of this law was to popularise Family Welfare/Family Planning Programme and which was also consistent with the National Population Policy it serves the purpose of the Act as mandated by the Constitution. The court further observed that this achieves a laudable purpose of social welfare and health care of the masses and is consistent with the National Population Policy provisions that "Demonstration of strong support to the small family norm, as well as personal example, by political, community, business, professional and religious leaders, media and film stars, sports personalities and opinion-makers, will enhance its acceptance throughout society."

There are important aspects of the spirit of the policy, for instance, in Para 6 that the policy "affirms the commitment of government towards voluntary and informed choice and consent of citizens while availing of the reproductive health care services and the continuation of the target free approach in administering Family Planning Services" and in Para 11 about forming of committees headed by elected women Panchayat members "to promote a gender standard for population stabilisation". These do not seem to have been placed for the consideration of the Supreme Court.

There are also other observations of the court, e.g. "the torrential increase in the population of the country is one of the major hindrances in the pace of India's socio-economic progress", reference to the example of China and that "complacence in controlling population in the name of democracy is too heavy a price to pay, allowing the nation to drift towards disaster", "who can better enable the discharge of functions and duties and such constitutional goals being achieved than the leaders of Panchayats themselves taking a lead and setting an example?" The Court also observed, "we don't think that with the awareness which is arising in the Indian womenfolk they are so helpless as to be compelled to bear a third child even though they do not wish to do so". The issues involved in these observations in the light of the experiences and limitations of the "population control" measures, the realities of Indian women's empowerment at the grassroot level and in different domains, from the public to the private, need to be submitted for the honourable court's consideration.

4

Case Studies

Our case studies show the experiences of Panchayat representatives, the practices adopted to circumvent the law and the anxiety and frustration of the affected persons who are caught in the complexity of the new law and the manipulations of their political opponents. Instances of sex selection tests, abortion of female foetus and completion of the pregnancy where the foetus was rightly or wrongly identified as male show the continuing prevalence of strong son preference and the potential of this law to further worsening of the adverse child sex ratio. The case studies are presented for each state but all the names have been changed to protect the identity of the respondents.

Malathi is around 29 years of age and has studied upto class IX. Her husband discontinued his education after intermediate (10 + 2) level. They belong to the Gowda caste (BC). They are residents of Nalgonda district of Andhra Pradesh. They have six acres of land which is rain-fed. They have three children: a son, 10 years old, studying in Class V; a daughter, 8 years old, studying in class I; another daughter, six years old studying in LKG class. Malathi's husband was interested in politics. He contested for the Sarpanch post in 1995 but lost. When the post of the Mandal Praja Territorial Committee member was declared as reserved for BC women in the 2001 elections, both husband and wife were keen to take the chance.

Malathi filed her nomination. Her opponents filed a complaint saying that her third child was born after May, 1995 and they produced a birth certificate given by the VAO, the local village official, showing her youngest child as two years old. So her nomination was rejected. Malathi said that she was angry and was disappointed when her nomination was rejected. She said that some big (rich) people, who have more than two children, have contested elections and are still continuing in the post by producing false certificates. She said that normally in rural areas people prefer to have more children and this affects those who have political aspirations. When she was told that it was not applicable to the MLAs and MPs, she questioned the discrimination and said that it was not justice, particularly to the poor sections and women.

Her nomination form was rejected on the report of the village official who reported that her daughter was two years old while in fact she was six years old and studying in LKG as the field team also noted. Malathi came to know about the law only when her nomination was rejected. She approached the Collector and showed her daughter to him but he expressed that he could not do anything in the matter. So she went to the Munsif's court and when it appeared that there too she would lose, she filed a case in the High Court, where it has been going on for the last 4-5 months. She has also undergone sterilization in 1996 after her third child. She says that she had spent a lot of money in preparing for the elections but her form was rejected as the village official was a sympathizer of her opponent's party. She questioned why such a law should have been brought in while the government says that women have been given one-third reservation and that they should come forward to use these reservations.

M. Madaniah, a 35 years old Sarpanch from the backward potter caste, won the election for the post from Nalgonda district in Andhra Pradesh in August 2001. Madaniah has four children from two wives. He knew about the two-child norm prior to the election. He made his first wife go for sterilization in 2000. He said that his electoral opponent who lost the election had got the birth date of his child changed in the Anganwari register, where it was entered only in pencil. Madaniah admits that he has four children, but that his second wife, mother of two of his children, is no more his wife as he had left her. He says that he had earlier married her, as the first wife did not have a child for two years.

The second wife also lives in the same village. He insists that he is not violating the two-child norm as he has left his second wife, the mother of two of his children. So the law did not make any impact of preventing further childbirth. The only consequence was of desertion of the second wife to circumvent the disqualification clause.

Maheshwari's husband was Upsarpanch in a Gram Panchayat in Andhra Pradesh in 1995–98 and became its Sarpanch in 1998. The couple had three children but all were born before the cut-off date. She became pregnant before the election. She underwent an abortion terminating her five-month old pregnancy because she wanted to stand for the post of Sarpanch in the Panchayat elections of 2001. This post had now become reserved for a backward class woman. She lost the election. Later, her two-year old son died when he accidentally drank kerosene. She denied the fact of abortion, perhaps fearing an inquiry. She was pregnant again at the time of our field work.

Nisha, educated up to Class VII, is from the backward potter caste and was elected as Sarpanch of her Gram Panchayat in Nalgonda district of Andhra Pradesh. She is a housewife. She got married when her husband was hardly 19 years old and she hardly 16 years old. By the age of 17 years she had her first child, a girl now 12 years old. The second is a boy now 9 years old and the third is also a boy now 7 years old. Nisha underwent tubectomy in 1994, well before the cut-off date. During 2000-2001, the state government was reprimanded by the High Court for delaying Panchayat elections which were to be held in May, 2000. The government had taken the plea that they had to decide about the reservations in Panchayats. Finally, a lottery system was followed to decide the reservations. In the lottery system the Sarpanch post in this GP got reserved for BC women. Since the beginning of the Panchayat Raj system, one family was continuously in the Sarpanch post in this Panchayat.

Nisha was active in SHGs in her village and was one of the educated women. She was the natural choice of the potter caste people who are in a majority in the village. She was also supported by the ruling party. The family, which was controlling the Panchayat for the last four decades, did not want to lose control. So, it supported one Lakshmi to contest the election and got the opposition party support for her. They thought that Nisha would not win the elections, so neither they nor anyone else raised any objection to Nisha's nomination which was accepted without any problem. So, in August, 2001, she was elected the Sarpanch of the GP in Nalgonda district with an absolute majority, defeating the candidate put up by the family who had till then always held the post of the Sarpanch in that Panchayat.

The problem started after the election results were announced. Nisha had won the election with a majority of 257 votes. Some people attacked Nisha during a victory procession organised by her supporters. Chilly powder was thrown in her face but this did not discourage her. She faced psychological harassment. She had to approach the police. Finally the matter ended in a compromise. But now the two-child norm law is being used against her. The powerful rivals were not willing to accept the victory of a BC woman with absolute majority only by the community's support. Her electoral rival filed a case against her in October, 2001 declaring falsely that Nisha's third child was born after May, 1995 though he was seven years old studying in Class I when the field team met Nisha. Everyone in the village knows that Lakshmi had neither the knowledge nor the money to defend the case in court. Nisha feels that rich politicians are misusing the two-child norm law to keep control and power in their hands.

She also feels that potential candidates, who are poor, will not be able to run around courts and spend money defending their cases, and this law is not in favour of the poor. She also feels that this law will discourage a lot of women in particular from entering politics because women are generally not encouraged to enter politics. The men will take this opportunity to further discourage women.

The court case is going on in the munsif's court. Nisha's husband engaged a lawyer and the reply was filed by him. It is to be seen how long the case drags on in the courts and how many times she has to run around courts and how much money will be spent on this. There is every possibility that sooner or later her husband will lose patience and may restrict her movements as she has also family responsibilities to look after, especially children. This will certainly have an adverse effect on other women not only of this village but also of other neighbouring villages.

Ramula SC is a former ward member of a Gram Panchayat in Mahboobnagar district of Andhra Pradesh. He is an agriculturist with less than one acre of land and with a reported annual income of about Rs. 10,000. He has four living children—one daughter and three sons, besides three children who died. His wife has undergone sterilization after the last child (aged 6 years now) was born as the doctor had advised that his wife would have problems if she had any more pregnancy.

He filed his nomination form in the elections in August, 2001 but the Mandal office advised him that it would be rejected because of the number of his children. His opponent also said that he would make a complaint about it. Hence, he did not file his nomination. Instead he put up his father as a candidate but he lost the election and another person, a BC candidate, was successful. He himself thus could not contest this election, as his last child was born one month after the grace period of one year (provided in the law) in 1995. He said, " *... I did whatever I could do as a ward member. I filed nomination also again. I was sure of winning... my opponents told me that they know that I will certainly win.... They threatened me that they will file a case against me.... I got angry ... I thought there will not be any use even if I win.... I thought that why should I run around courts... we are daily wage earners... why take the trouble.... I made my father contest the election... but he lost the election...we didn't expect the fourth child as there was eight-year gap after the third child... it was accidental....*".

Despite being a ward member from 1995, he came to have the knowledge about this law only in the 2001 election. In this village, another candidate too wanted to file his nomination for ward member from the same seat. He was also similarly advised by the Mandal office people. So he too did not file his nomination paper and filed the nomination of his old mother. She was elected and also became the Upsarpanch. So this law shifted the candidature from the younger aspiring persons to the older generation of their parents whose number of children born before 1995 do not create a disqualification under the two-child norm law. The case illustrates how the law is denying the opportunity of contesting election to the younger members of this social group.

Romaiah, a 36 years old SC graduate, was a Mandal Council Member (Councillor) in Nalgonda district of Andhra Pradesh in 1987 and again since 1995. In the year 2001, he contested and won election again. He has two daughters and one son who is the youngest and is six years old. His wife underwent sterilization in 1997. He received a notice about his having three children. He has replied to the notice and intends to stress that the third child was born in 1995. He was in the Mandal as member since 1995 but the complaint has been made only after his winning the election in 2001. He belongs to the opposition party. The complainant is from the ruling party. He feels that insistence on the compliance of this law is only party politics. Those who are in power are not affected. Others are affected more and the complaints are made mainly against them. It appears that the ruling party is better organised to use this law against others. He said "*... a case was filed against me in November, 2001 alleging that I have three children... the Act is not good. This is democracy.... I have the right to have children.... I got angry and argued that this Act should apply to the MLAs and MPs also.... Pressure should not be put on people... all those who realise and are convinced are going for family planning anyway...people elect because candidates are good... by which Act they can be removed? ... cases should not be filed after one gets elected... the Act is being misused by the political opponents only to settle political scores...*"

Somyajulu, a 40 years old cobbler, belongs to the Scheduled Caste and is educated up to Class III. He was a Sarpanch in Nalgonda district in Andhra Pradesh from 1995 to 2001. He has two acres of land and a well, which irrigates one crop in a year. Besides agriculture, both Somyajulu and his wife work in a stone quarry when there is no agricultural work. They have three children aged 12, 10 and 6 years; the first two go to school. He was elected as Sarpanch under SC reservation and was supported by the Congress Party. His wife became pregnant for the third time in 1997 and a complaint was lodged against him. He approached persons in an NGO for help and told them how he could contest the election with the support of some local people and how after changing their party, the same people had made a complaint against him as he had refused to join their new party.

Somyajulu along with an NGO official and a Dalit leader went to the authorities with a plea that he was being falsely implicated as he had refused to join the party of those who had lodged the complaint. They also met the opposition party leaders and told them that they had collected information about their party people who had more than three children and could implicate their party candidates on the basis of this evidence and make the same allegation as they had of not following the two-child norm. The divisional level opponent leaders compromised and the complaint against Somyajulu was not pursued seriously.

Somyajulu also used the strategy of ensuring that any inquiry team would not be able to see his pregnant wife. He sent his wife away to her parents' home for two years. So when the officials came to inquire about the number of his children they could not get any proof and left. When the local people asked him about his wife, he told them that she was sick and getting treatment in Hyderabad. In the meantime he quietly married another younger girl. He had a son from his second wife also who was about one and a half years old at the time of our fieldwork.

Vasanthi is around 28 years of age and has studied up to Class X. She belongs to the Gowda caste (BC). For the last 50 years her husband's family is in politics. Her father-in-law was continuously Sarpanch Gram Panchayat till 1995. Vasanthi was elected as Sarpanch of the Gram Panchayat in Rangareddi district of Andhra Pradesh in the August, 2001 elections under BC woman reservation. Her husband was Sarpanch till August, 2001. Financially, they are well-off. The husband is running wine shops and the family has substantial agricultural land. They have three children—a daughter, 11 years old, who is in Class V; a son who is 8 years old and is in Class II; and the youngest son, 7 years old, is in KG. Vasanthi says that she underwent family planning operation in 1994.

The state government reserved this Gram Panchayat for BC women for the August, 2001 elections. Naturally Vasanthi contested the elections and won with 900 votes. Her opponent who got 500 votes filed a case against her citing violation of the two-child norm law.

Vasanthi received a notice about violation of the two-child norm and the reply was to be filed by the end of January, 2002. She produced her child's birth certificate and the certificate of the family planning operation in 1994. She said, "*...I got family planning operation done in 1994... because we wanted a small family... not because of elections.... my opponents belonging to the BJP filed a case against me... the Act should apply to N.T. Rama Rao and Lalu Prasad also.*"

There is another angle to this case. When her husband was the Sarpanch, a complaint was also filed against him on the ground of violation of the two-child norm. But he completed his term.

Vasanthi explains the prevalent situation when she discusses the complaint against two other Panchayat representatives about violating the two-child norm. She says that the complaint cannot achieve anything. The persons who have received notices about such violation will be able to continue for their five-year tenure. The complaint was made about her husband violating the norm when only one year was left of his tenure as Sarpanch. Notice of inquiry came from the district Panchayat Officer's office but her husband was able to manage it and hence no notice came from the court.

As an Anganwari worker informed our team, though reluctantly, *"the sarpanch had his youngest child in 1999 but he managed the case by paying a bribe. Now his wife is the Sarpanch and they will manage in the same manner again. They have perhaps kept the child in Hyderabad. In fact the statement about the sterilization operation is also questionable"*. It is the story of powerful, resourceful persons able to manage the complaints, cases, etc.

Archna Devi, 35 years old, illiterate scheduled caste Sarpanch from Faridabad district in Haryana, works as a wage labourer. Her illiterate husband works as a mason. She contested the Panchayat election in 2000 and was elected from a seat reserved for the scheduled caste. She gave birth to her eighth child when she was holding the post of Sarpanch. When she received the disqualification notice she did not contest it. She said that she did not feel angry when she was removed from the post of Sarpanch, "*What anger can a poor person show? It does not matter if the Sarpanch post has gone. I was working as a wage labourer before, so do I now.*"

She is aware of the family planning methods and uses Mala-D, she says. The reason for her giving birth to a third son after the cut-off date was not only due to her own desire but also because the family pressure had mounted on her despite the fact that she already had two sons. Another reason was that her eldest son is disabled and so not helpful to her in the manual wage work. Hence, there was a desire for another son. She said *"Daughters were born in the process of wanting sons."* She says that women have no freedom in deciding the number of children the family should have. People go for sex determination examination and for induced abortion if it is not a son, she adds. Other villagers also say that they have heard about these tests but nobody discloses the facts.

Banta Singh, 35 years old, Class VIII pass, OBC is a Panch in the Gram Panchayat in Ambala district of Haryana. He had three daughters and one son and his last issue was the son. He was disqualified as the last child was born after the cut-off date in 1995. His wife underwent sterilization operation in 2000 but after he had already been disqualified. He says that she went for sterilization to limit the family size after they had a son for which he had family pressure as well as his own inclination. So when the notice came about his having four children he admitted this and consequently was removed.

Banta Singh was elected unanimously in the 2000 election and the community had agreed that the issue of his violation of the two-child norm would not be raised. But the opposition party people complained about his four children when he went with other Panchayat people to remove their encroachment on the Panchayat land.

We can see in this case the strong desire for a son and the attitude of the people adopting family planning including sterilization but after achieving their desired family size or after having a son. It also shows that the issue of the "Norm" and the law has not been seen as relevant in the people's reproductive decisions.

The case of **Jagmal,** a Meo Sarpanch of a Village Panchayat, Gurgaon district of Haryana gives interesting insights. He is 42 years old and illiterate. He was a Panch earlier in 1988 and was elected as a Sarpanch in February, 2000. He has eight surviving children, aged two to 22 years. Earlier, his three children died after birth. His youngest child is a boy born in 1999 after the two-child norm became effective. He had a vague idea about the new law. "The BDO had told us before the election that one should not have more than two children after 1995 which I could not understand correctly", he said. Of his eight children, six are daughters and two are sons. He says that he himself wanted two sons and that is why he has so many children. He was elected in March 2000 and complaints started within two days. The Deputy Commissioner then removed him from the post within six months. But the Commissioner gave a stay order. Then the High Court rejected the case. So he moved the Supreme Court, where he was given a "stay" pending final decision.

Jagmal engaged five eminent lawyers in his case. He raised the issue of his religion, which does not favour family planning, also that the MPs/MLAs and government servants had not been brought under this law, that those who were framing the laws themselves had more children and the Panchayat representatives were being subjected to a law made by them. After he obtained a stay order from the Supreme Court, a number of other cases were also filed in the Supreme Court and stay orders were granted in those cases too, on similar grounds. While he himself does not say about not contesting the Panchayat election if he had known about the law, others state that they would not have contested had they been told about the law before the contest.

Jagmal's attitude seems to be casual about the family size and about the Panchayats. His statement about religion, about discrimination, application of the two-child norm to Panchayats only seems to be a repetition of what his counsels prepared for the court case. It seems that in this area the family planning services and contact-and-visits approach by the health workers have not been very effective. Further, the reaction of the affected persons still does not indicate that this law makes them think about the family size issue as was expected by those who proposed this law.

Karim, 40 years old, a Meo, is a Higher Secondary pass Sarpanch of a Gram Panchayat in Faridabad district of Haryana. He was a Panch in 1995 and contested for the post of Sarpanch in the election held in February, 2000. He is an agriculturist owning 10 acres of irrigated land. He is aware of the family planning methods and says that his wife uses Mala-D for spacing children. Though he does not desire to have additional children but he did not allow his wife to go for sterilization because he does not want to completely stop childbirth. He has four children (three sons and one daughter). His fourth child—a son—was born after the cut-off date, i.e. after 1995, and is seven years old. He had concealed this fact and had given false information that the child was born before 1995. Generally on the basis of the declaration given at the time of election no scrutiny is done of the facts submitted and no one had objected about his giving false information.

Banta Singh, a 60 years old villager, and others made a complaint that Karim's fourth child was born after 1995 (but they did not indicate the exact date). Then they complained again after collecting facts from the village chowkidar who maintains the birth and death records and also getting facts from the CMO's office. Consequently Karim received a show-cause notice after remaining in office for six months. He was removed by the Deputy

Commissioner (DC). A bye-election was held for the post vacated by Karim before the completion of six months after his disqualification. His opponent, Banta Singh, contested for this post and was declared elected. In the meantime Karim went to the High Court and not getting any stay from there he filed a writ petition in the Supreme Court and got a stay order. He did not hand over the charge to Banta Singh. On the basis of the stay order, DC allowed him to continue in the post of the Sarpanch held by him. So he was continuing in his post when our team met him.

Karim was under tension when he received the show-cause notice and when he was removed by the DC. He did not mention the amount but says that he spent a lot of money on this litigation. He says that people go for sex-determination tests and get abortion done if it is not a son and escape disqualification but this is not permitted in Islam. He further said that this type of talk about pre-natal diagnostic test, abortion, etc., is a common talk in the village Chaupal. Another villager also corroborated this fact. Though the details of cases of sex determination and abortion are not openly revealed but this is a fact which cannot be denied, they said.

Manjeet Singh is a SC Panch of a Gram Panchayat in Ambala district of Haryana and has studied up to Class VII and has three children. His youngest child is only three years old. He has been disqualified because he had the third child after 1995. He says he had told about his children at the time of the election. Had he known about the two-child law he would not have contested. He had two daughters, so he himself wanted a son. He was removed on the complaint of the person who had contested election against him. He did not even try to move a court and obtain a stay order because it costs at least Rs. 5,000 which he could not afford. A very old person has become a Panch in his place.

Mohan Lal, 35 years old, Valmiki Sarpanch in Ambala district of Haryana, worked as a sweeper. He received the disqualification notice because people complained that he had four children—three daughters and one son. But he said that the fact was that he had only one daughter and that the other three children were of his brother. He had added their names to his ration-card to get extra sugar and kerosene. He has now made a separate ration card. His case was still pending before the Deputy Commissioner at the time of our study. He said that he only wants one more child now and that too a son. Others who have agricultural land may want more children but he is a sweeper. His wife is also a sweeper. They do not want a large family.

Smt. Kamlesh, 26, OBC, is a Panch in a Gram Panchayat in Faridabad district of Haryana. She is Class VI pass and is a housewife. Her husband is a matriculate and works in a factory. She contested the Panchayat election for the first time in 2000. She has four children—all sons—of whom the youngest is one year old and was born after the cut-off date. The eldest is nine years old. She had given birth to two more children—both daughters—who expired soon after their birth. They were from her second and third pregnancies. She is aware of the family planning methods and uses Copper-T to prevent further pregnancy.

She was disqualified three months back after remaining in office for only one and a half years on the complaint of her opponent in the election who was defeated by her. As stated by her, a well-to-do OBC Zamindar, of this Gram Panchayat, got a certificate from the CMO that she had only two children. He had assured her that he would help her in fighting her case in the court. She was not inclined to go to court as she was poor and would not be able to afford the cost of litigation. She had felt very bad and was anguished when she received the notice and when disqualified after inquiry. She was very sour that there were other Panchayat members in the same Gram Panchayat who had violated the two-child norm after the cut-off date but were not removed because no one had made any complaint against them. She also gave their names. In all the cases the last child was born after 1995. Feeling sad about her removal she said, *"I was removed on a complaint made out of jealousy. My opponent had also done mischief at the time of election."*

Shivendra, 33 years old, a graduate, is Sarpanch in a Gram Panchayat in Faridabad district of Haryana. He is an agriculturist and had contested the Panchayat election for the second time in

2000. He has four children (two sons and two daughters). On a complaint made by the villagers about his having violated the two-child norm, he received a show-cause notice twice from the SDM. The SDM himself came for inquiry .The dispute was whether the last child was born after the cut-off date as the complaint alleged or the child (seven years old) was born before 1995 as Shivendra had claimed. The SDM obtained the details about the family members and had taken a copy of the admission certificate from the school he had attended. Shivendra read in a local newspaper that he was being removed from the post of the Sarpanch, so he became active and got a stay order from the Commissioner.

When he received the notice, he was very much perturbed and tense. He said *"There was a marriage in the village and the Barat procession was coming, so I felt ashamed before them. Therefore I was even more angry."* It disturbed him more because the complaint was false and motivated and was by his opponent who was defeated in the Panchayat election. He mentioned two cases of persons in his Gram Panchayat who had violated the two-child norm but were continuing in their positions because nobody had complained against them.

He was aware of the contraceptive methods and had his wife go for sterilization since he was not keen to have any more children. This he did after having two sons. He said, *"I wanted two sons, because I am alone. This is why I wanted more children."*

He stated that the notice was received by him after one year of his working as Sarpanch. He got a stay order from the Commissioner by engaging a lawyer for Rs. 5,000. He expressed his feelings with anguish. *"This rule is wrong because the government has not made any publicity of the law. This legislation is good because there will be a check on the population growth, but this infringes on the fundamental rights of the people."* Lastly, he says that he has a grudge against the law being discriminatory and about the action being taken on false complaints by others who only want to settle scores with their opponents.

Virumal, a 31 years old male Panch in a Gram Panchayat in Ambala district of Haryana, has studied up to Class V. He has three children, of whom the youngest is three years old, and was born after 1995. His wife had a family planning operation in 2000 because they wanted to limit the family size. He was not interested in the post of the Panch. He was asked to contest by others just 10 minutes before the nomination time. He says that had he known about the law he would not have contested. He was removed by a order of the Deputy Commissioner and a 70 years old person was elected to fill the vacancy.

Gurdeep, a male Panch, of the same Gram Panchayat, has studied up to Class X and has two daughters. He also has one son who was born after 1995. He too says that had he been told that not even one of the three children should have been born after 1995, he would not have contested the election. Even as the other Panch in his Gram Panchayat, who was also removed, stated, he was not bothered. After all he was not getting any salary which he was going to lose. He said, *"I was furious as to why such a law was enacted. Those persons who receive a salary may be afraid of this law. We are not afraid, we are not getting any salary."*

These two elected Panches of Gram Panchayat who were removed show no regret or disappointment at their removal. They also say that they would not have contested had they known about the law.

Bhola aged 42 years is a Sarpanch of a Gram Panchayat in Betul district of Madhya Pradesh. He has studied up to Class V and belongs to the Gond community (ST). He is a very popular person in his tribal village. He contested the Panchayat election for the first time for the post of Sarpanch when this seat became reserved for a ST candidate. He defeated four persons who contested against him. He claims his victory was due to his popularity as a religious preacher and an expert exorcist. He obliges people with his services to cure their ailments or to solve their other problems. He attends to the Panchayat work and knows how to get development programmes approved and executed.

His wife aged 35 years is also literate. They have nine children (five sons and four daughters), the eldest is 18 years and the youngest are twins (a son and a daughter) about 10 months old.

He knows about family planning but does not believe in practising it. He has a belief that if he practises family planning methods, his family deity would get annoyed and the power of exorcism and his being a religious preacher will be ineffective.

He had seven children when he contested the Panchayat election in January/February 2000. When asked about his awareness of the legislation of two-child norm, his reply was in the affirmative since the Panchayat secretary had told him about it. Undeterred about the consequences, he asserted, *"People have elected me, so I will continue to serve them. If I am removed from the post due to the legislation, I will definitely go to court."* His stock reply was that he is for the service of the people both as a Sarpanch and as a healer as he is elected by them. He does not consider this legislation good as this will deny the right to contest Panchayat elections, especially the poor. Obviously his leadership will not change even if the legislation leads to his disqualification. His case shows the need for efforts for more education, for addressing superstitions and practices in the tribal areas to enable them to make more informed choices about their family and their future.

Hirulal, 36 years old Sarpanch on a reserved seat for the Scheduled Caste in a Gram Panchayat in Hoshangabad district of Madhya Pradesh, contested the Panchayat election in January, 2000 for the first time. He had three children (two sons and one daughter) before he contested the Panchayat election. His fourth child, a son, was born on 7 May, 2001. He received a show-cause notice on 18 March, 2002 for violating the two-child norm.

Hirulal was unaware of the legislation which was enacted in May, 2000, but learnt of it when it became effective from 26 January, 2001. His wife was five months pregnant then. Determined not to lose his Panchayat post, he planned to abort the pregnancy. He was desperate and wanted to do whatever was possible to avoid disqualification due to the birth of his additional child. He consulted the doctor in the nearby PHC who in turn advised him to consult another doctor in Hoshangabad. The latter did not agree to do induced abortion at such an advanced stage of pregnancy because of the risk involved for the pregnant woman and the likely legal action. So the son was born and made his father liable for disqualification. He submitted an application to the state government that his wife became pregnant in August 2000, i.e. six months before the effective date of this legislation (26 January, 2001) and hence it was not a violation of the two-child norm and has made an appeal to exempt him. He had also not given up the option to go to court.

Hirulal considers the post of Sarpanch as a prize possession which has come to him due to the reservation under the Panchayat Act but feels cheated under the same Act for facing the trauma of disqualification.

Kallu, a SC aged 35 years, is a Ward Panch in a single habitation Gram Panchayat with a population of about 2,500 in Vidisha district of Madhya Pradesh. The Gram Panchayat has a mixed population of Dangi, Kirar, Rajput, Brahmin and Harijans with predominance of the Dangis and Kirar who are OBC. The Gram Panchayat is very well connected by road. It has 15 elected Panchayat representatives with five women members. Kallu is illiterate and earns his living by grazing village cows and buffaloes and supplements his earning by working as a wage labourer. His wife and his eldest son (only 10 years old) also work as wage labourers. Their combined income still keeps them below the poverty line. He has four children—two sons, aged 10 years and 2 months, and two daughters aged 7 years and 3 years. The youngest son was born in August, 2001.

As his Panchayat ward became reserved for SC, he was encouraged by the village Patel and other persons of the village to contest election. He had been observing other Panchayat members elected during the first Panchayat election of 1994. He too wanted to do development work in the village, especially in his ward. So he readily filed his nomination papers in the election in January/ February, 2000. There were two other candidates. He mobilised people to vote for him and in this process spent about Rs. 3,000 borrowed from a moneylender. He has repaid the amount from his wages and those of his ten years old son.

After winning the election Kallu is actively involved in the

Panchayat work. He cites some of the development work done due to his persuasive efforts. Being illiterate he is not much aware about the rules and regulations and instructions issued from time to time. When asked whether he was aware about the two-child norm, he expressed ignorance. It was a shock to him to know that the birth of his youngest son on 10 August, 2001 could disqualify him for the post of the Panch. He or any one else had not received any notice about the violation of the two-child norm when the field team met him.

He said that instructions had not been received in the Panchayat and the Sarpanch or other members too had not even discussed this point in any Panchayat meeting. He says that he has adopted family planning methods for limiting his family size. He observed that "this reservation provided to the poor like me will get negated due to this legislation. What is the good of it"? In case he is removed, he does not intend fighting his case. He also remarked that this legislation will not help in population control.

This case shows the type of persons likely to face the impact of this legislation—the poor, the illiterate, the weaker sections—who enter Panchayats for the first time but whose preference is still not of a family of two children as even his 10 years old son works as a wage labourer. Education for his children and better livelihood will help him. The fact that he borrowed money to contest election, which he repaid with his own and his son's wages, shows that he was a serious contestant and his disqualification will be a really hard blow demotivating him forever.

Kamta aged 30 years contested and was elected for the post of a Panch in his Gram Panchayat in Betul district in MP when his ward was reserved for ST candidates in the Panchayat elections of 2000. His father is the Sarpanch of the same Panchayat. He has studied up to Class X. With landed property of 15 acres of irrigated land, the joint family makes an annual earning of Rs. 25,000. His wife is illiterate and has no interest or involvement in politics. They have three children. The third child was born after the cut-off date of 26 January, 2001 for disqualification for violation of the two-child norm in this state's Panchayat law.

He was very much aware of the two-child norm legislation.

When asked why he did not keep a check on the number of children, he said that it was their planned move to have three or more children, because, as he explained, his elder brother does not have any issue. So he planned to give at least one or two children to his brother in adoption. He is not deterred because of the likely disqualification. He will get things settled well in time. He was proud to say that his wife was pregnant again and thus they expect an additional child as well. After this child he will get himself operated. About this legislation, he said that it was good from the point of population control but the poor and the downtrodden would be the most affected.

The wife of **Mangatram,** Sarpanch of a Gram Panchayat in Morena district in Madhya Pradesh, gave birth to a third child in November, 2001. He maintained that the child could not be his as his wife was away at her parents' home in Uttar Pradesh since November, 1999. He requested the ADM for permission to divorce his wife on grounds of adultery (as reported in a Hindi daily *Nav Bharat,* Bhopal edition dated 16 April, 2002). The compulsions of the norm are leading to such a practice and allegations so derogatory to women, when the husband, a sitting Sarpanch, wants to prevent his own disqualification.

Mohini, a Scheduled Caste Sarpanch of a Gram Panchayat in Sehore district in Madhya Pradesh, succumbed to the family pressure to have a son since she had two daughters and gave birth to a third child, a daughter, after the cut-off date. The couple had given away their second daughter in adoption to Mohini's brother to circumvent the disqualification clause but this plea was not accepted in court. Mohini's case shows the ground realities of the family pressure for a son and the inability of the woman to resist such pressures despite the impact of women's empowerment and their new public role.

Ramprakash, aged 42 years, a tribal Sarpanch in Betul in Madhya Pradesh, has six children (four daughters and two sons) through three wives. The first wife died but the two wives are alive. His Gram Panchayat of five villages is located in a Gond tribal tract and is in a Schedule V area where, under the Panchayats

Extension to Scheduled Areas Act 1996 provisions, all the Sarpanches and Chairpersons of Panchayats at all levels have to be tribals only. Ramprakash's last child, a boy, was born in February, 2001. We interviewed Ramprakash when cases of disqualification under the two-child norm had not started in this state. So, when asked about the two-child norm, he took this very lightly and said that he had heard about it from the Panchayat secretary. When informed that he was subject to disqualification because of his son, he replied: *"The Sarpanch's post is not going to support me during my old age, but my son will. That is why I had an additional child due to my desire for a son. It does not really matter if I lose the post of the Sarpanch."* His third wife aged 25 years has undergone sterilization after the birth of the male child who is her only issue. At the time of our study there were a number of such cases of violation of the norm but no action had been initiated.

Sarupi Bai, 30 years old and illiterate, is a Panch in a Gram Panchayat in Sehore district in Madhya Pradesh. She contested for the first time on a seat reserved for the ST. Her husband, 35 years old is literate. Both are agricultural labourers. They have five children (four sons and one daughter), the eldest is 10 years old daughter and the youngest is a son who is two years old.

The couple was unaware of the family planning methods and they never practised any of the methods. After the last child was born, Sarupi Bai went for sterilisation. Only after, she learnt about the Sarpanch of this Gram Panchayat receiving a show-cause notice for violation of the two-child norm, she came to know that there was this two-child law for Panchayats. She was happy that she was not affected as her last son was born before 26 January, 2001. But she does not consider the law as good and says *"Harijan/ Adivasis have been given the benefit of reservations but they will not get this benefit if they are removed under this law."*

When the need to have a small family was explained to her she said, *"People give birth to more children so that at least some will survive in the event of death of one or two of them"*. She cited the case of one Leela Bai who went for sterilization after she gave birth to two children (both sons). Unfortunately one child was drowned in the village well and the other died due to illness. This is why Sarupi Bai says that she went for sterilization only after having five children.

This unfortunate incident in a nearby village, though a rare case, has scared the people who take initiative for family planning operation. What is needed here is education, strengthening of health-care services and counselling for adoption of the small family norm and not a law for disqualification from Panchayats.

Sushma, aged 25 years, a SC, who has studied up to Class VII and has three sons, got elected to the post of Sarpanch in the Village Panchayat in Vidisha district in Madhya Pradesh in 2000 when it was reserved for SC women. Her husband encouraged her to contest. He helped her in filing the nomination papers. She claims to have spent about Rs. 10,000 in contesting the election. She is active, holds monthly meetings regularly and participates fully in all the activities. She has to her credit completion of a number of development works in the Gram Panchayat. Villagers are happy with the consequent adequate supply of drinking water, good village roads, schooling facilities, etc.

Sushma has three children, all sons aged four years, two-and-a-half years and three months. She was not aware of the two-child norm legislation. She said that she had not received any such instructions from government authorities. She was taken aback when she was told that the birth of her third son (about three months old at the time of the interview) after 26 January, 2001 could disqualify her for holding the office of Sarpanch. Nobody had reported the matter nor had anybody questioned her. She, however, reacted very sharply about the legislation having been made applicable to the Panchayats only and not to MPs and MLAs.

She said, *"33 per cent reservation for women will become a mere unfulfilled promise. If not for awareness, the government should have at least given intimation about this legislation. Society condemns a woman as 'inauspicious', 'immoral' if she gives birth to female children as every man desires to have a son. Therefore I do not think that this legislation will have any impact on the population growth."*

This couple practises family planning to limit their family size and for spacing children on their own as mentioned by her. She had the third child as she wanted to have a daughter after her two sons but her desire could not be fulfilled as the third issue was also a male child. Now she does not want to have any more children. She intended to go to court if she faced a case for disqualification. She had not received any notice up to the time of the field work in the first phase when the field team met her.

This case shows how this two-child law will deny political participation to new emerging women's leadership from the weaker sections which are performing well. Secondly, people like her are already deciding to adopt family planning when their desired family size is complete. The disqualification will only bring disappointment and frustration to these sections which are not aware of the new law, but are adopting contraceptives though after they had their desired family size.

Shailbala's case was the first case of violation of the two-child norm in the state of Madhya Pradesh and was reported in the state media (*Nai Dunia,* Hindi daily, Bhopal) on 1 November, 2001. Shailbala was the Sarpanch of the Gram Panchayat in Neemuch district. The Collector gave her notice to disqualify her for violating the two-child norm. She is about 35 years old and had two daughters aged 10 and 4 years when she contested the Panchayat election in February, 2000. She has studied up to Class X. She gave birth to a son in September, 2001. Hardly one month after this birth, about 10-15 villagers reported the matter to the Collector, requesting for her removal.

The Sarpanch seat of this Gram Panchayat was earlier held by a male as it was unreserved then. It became reserved for women in 2000. Shailbala was elected by defeating eight opponents who included the former Sarpanch's wife. This former Sarpanch is now the Upsarpanch.

In our interview, Shailbala and her husband stated that she was not in fact subject to disqualification as the first child—a daughter—was adopted by them and was in fact the daughter of her maternal uncle who was residing in Ajmer. This was because her maternal uncle had five daughters with no male issue and she had not given birth to any child for a long time after her marriage at the age of 18 years. Later in reply to the notice from the Collector, she took the plea that she had given her one daughter in adoption. Obviously she has a third child—a son—whom she wanted and now she finds that this deprives her of a post she won after a keen contest against the wife of the former Sarpanch.

The couple suspect that the complaint is the mischief of the ex-Sarpanch (now Upsarpanch) who was removed earlier within three years of his tenure as Sarpanch for misuse of powers. Since he got elected as Upsarpanch in 2000, he was power hungry and mobilised some people and lodged a complaint of violation of the two-child norm by the present woman Sarpanch. She and her husband intended to fight the case in all the legal fora.

This case shows three trends, which are also observed in other states. First, the two-child norm clause is used by political opponents to settle scores and move petitions or file complaints. Second, the first victims are invariably the weaker sections and women—an OBC woman in this case. Third, those with resources fight the cases and also try to prove that they were still qualified like Shailbala who said that her first daughter was adopted by her or that she had given one daughter in adoption, etc., and still think of going to the High Court and Supreme Court.

Shikha, 25 years old, SC Sarpanch in Bhopal district of Madhya Pradesh, contested the reserved seat for SC women as a new entrant to grassroot politics. She is an illiterate housewife. Her husband is Class X pass and besides pursuing agricultural occupation having 40 acres of agricultural land, actively participates in politics.

She has three daughters, the third born in February, 2002. This made her liable for disqualification for violation of the two-child norm. She says that jealousy and rivalry are common features in villages and in grassroots politics as she had experienced during the last one-and-a-half years of her Panchayat work. So the rival group with the Upsarpanch as the main brain behind it, got the opportunity to settle an old score with her. They reported the birth of her third child to the Collector, Bhopal, and requested for her removal for violating the two-child norm.

She is not aware of family planning methods and has never practised any to limit the family size. Her husband had two daughters from his first wife who is no more. She too had two daughters before she contested the election. So there was family pressure to have at least one son in the family. She became aware of the legislation of the two-child norm when she was in the sixth month of pregnancy in November, 2001. She said, *"I myself would have gone for abortion to avoid disqualification, but being a woman I did not have the freedom in a joint family to do so, nor does any other woman like me enjoy such freedom."*

Shikha was very upset when she learnt that the show-cause notice had been issued to her by the Collector, though she said she had undertaken various development works in the village like construction of village roads, repair of school building, etc. and completed them. On knowing about the show-cause notice being served on her, her husband became active and consulted lawyers to find out ways to save his wife from disqualification. Not taking any chance, they had also given away their second daughter in adoption to Shikha's brother. Shikha later got a stay order from the court where her case was pending.

Asha Malik, 31 years old, is SC Sarpanch in the Gram Panchayat in Cuttack district of Orissa. She was elected in the 1997 election. She was disqualified in March, 2000. She had claimed that her youngest child was born two years before the election and produced a birth certificate from a PHC in Ganjam district where her natal family lives. It was, however, not accepted and she was removed from the post. During the discussions she said the age of her youngest child was six years but after checking with her husband, said it was seven years.

It was obvious that the proceedings for her disqualification, the inquiry and the case in the High Court had left her quite traumatised. She was reluctant even to speak to our team and said so in so many words. Even her family members, the husband, mother-in-law, father-in-law and sister-in-law, had to be convinced that the field team was only a research team and not doing any "inquiry". They told us that there was too much of "questioning" in the court and she had had a lot of psychological problems because of this experience and, therefore, she did not even keep good health. She had earlier pursued the case in the High Court for seven months. In the meantime the Collector removed her from the post.

The Collector had in fact suspended her in March, 2000. The case in the High Court lasted for two years from 1998. She obtained a stay order in October, 2001. In the mean time bye-election had been held and one old lady was elected as Sarpanch. When she won the case in the High Court, she went back to take charge. But the newly elected Sarpanch did not hand over charge. She got an order from the Collector that the charge should be given back to her in 24 hours.

Others in the village spoke of how the local power politics of the BJP and Congress Party worked in this case. Whoever was more influential was able to put pressure and get a false certificate from a doctor. Asha got the certificate from Berhampur. The complainants got a certificate from the local PHC but they could not substantiate it. Her three children's names and details are entered in the local PHC but even then the complainants were not able to obtain the correct information. The villagers also alleged that the Sarpanch had spent about Rs. 30,000 in the court cases and so was able to get a stay order. The complainants did not have so much money.

So we see the extent of financial resources used in contesting these cases to finally win cases and also how this causes tension, anxiety and leaves psychological effects on the candidates and on their families.

Kavita Mohanty was 35 years old and Sarpanch of a Gram Panchayat in Orissa. She was educated up to Class XI. Her third child was born after the two-child norm became applicable, but she was elected to the post in 1997 and continued up to August, 2000 as her party was in power. According to her, when a new political party came to power in the state in 1999, political pressure was brought on the Divisional Commissioner to initiate action against her, since she belonged to the opposition party.

Twenty-six years old **Menka,** a Sarpanch in a Gram Panchayat in Angul district in Orissa, belonged to a scheduled tribe. She had three daughters, one of them born after the cut-off date for the two-child norm disqualification in the state law. She had not used any contraceptives nor gone for sterilisation, as she wanted a son. During the third pregnancy, she had gone for sex determination test and the doctor had told her that she was carrying a son. This led to her carrying the pregnancy to full term. The irony was that the third child that was identified as a male foetus turned out to be a girl. "If I had known this, I would have aborted. Now I have lost my position and also there is no son", was all she could say. She tried to prevent her disqualification by getting a certificate that her child was that of her sister but the Collector did not accept her plea.

Radha, a 30 years old scheduled caste woman, was elected a Panch in a Gram Panchayat in Angul district of Orissa in 1997. She and her husband are engaged in making leaf cups and plates. During her fourth pregnancy, when she was already a Panch, she undertook a sex determination test and was told that the foetus was a female. She had an abortion. In her next pregnancy, she had the test done again and learnt that it was a male. She continued the pregnancy and delivered her fourth child, a son, and hence faced removal from the post. For her having a son was more important than the political post.

She had four months of her tenure left when she was removed. She told the District Collector that since so many other Panchayat members also had four children they too should be removed. She was told that there were no complaints against them. In her case the BDO had conducted the inquiry and verified the facts from the Anganwari records. She stated that the complaint against her and one other Ward Panch was made by the male Panchayat secretary as she, along with the village people, had got him removed for misappropriating funds of the monthly remuneration of the Ward Panches. However, her having the additional child, a son, gave the Panchayat secretary the opportunity to take revenge.

Sanjay Malik, 31 years, Matric, OBC Sarpanch of Gram Panchayat in Dhenkanal district of Orissa, had three children, all daughters. He has been removed from his post. He is bitter. He says, *"If I had known earlier, I would not have contested election. I won by the highest number of votes in Dhenkanal and I have also been given a scroll of honour. Should we leave India because we have more than two children? I felt angry about the law as I was removed after winning the election. I had planned what work I would do in the Panchayat in five years".*

He went to the court of Sub-Judge but lost and then to the High Court where also he lost. Then a member of the opposite party was elected in his place in 1998. He does not agree with the rationale of this law and says that, *"First we should spread education and then only make a law."*

He narrates why he has been removed. *"I was not on good terms with the Zila Parishad. That is why a complaint was made against me. Otherwise I would not have lost the post of Sarpanch. What is the use of making such a law? Now I have lost. Now I can have five children. How will government prevent it now?"*

Malik contested the election despite being legally ineligible. He already had more than two children. He did not consider it a serious matter. Others also did not raise the issue. The complaint was made when his relations with the Zila Parishad became strained. In the meantime his work was recognised. Action for his removal has only made him bitter. Our visit to the Panchayat area showed his considerable following and respect. A young, bright, potential younger leader has been thus lost for the Panchayats in this process.

Shailja Pradhan, ST female Sarpanch in a Gram Panchayat in Angul district of Orissa, is 26 years old and has three daughters. The last two daughters were born after the cut-off date for disqualification. One of them was born after she was elected in 1997 and this being the third child led to her disqualification. She has not used any contraceptives or gone for sterilization, as she wanted to have a son.

Her in-laws narrated how she was very upset and cried at the birth of her third daughter because after the sex determination test which she had quietly undergone, the doctor had told her that she was carrying a son. This she had told her in-laws also. Had the doctor told her that it was a female, she would have gone for induced abortion. Her case shows that the law is also leading to sex-selective abortions though people do not easily admit or discuss this issue.

She tried to prevent her being disqualified by getting a certificate that her child was that of her sister but the Deputy Collector did not accept it. She knew about the law even before the election and she had the third child because she was told by the doctor that it would be a male child.

Surekha Bhoi, 28 years old, Scheduled Caste Panch of a Gram Panchayat in Cuttack district, was elected in 1997. She and her husband work as wage labourers. She has passed Class V. She has two living children—one son and one daughter. She says that she does not want more children but she neither knows nor practises any family planning method. She had a third child who died at the age of one month only four-five months ago. So she would have been subject to disqualification if the child had survived. The law speaks of not more than two living children. She does not even express awareness of the legislation. *"We do not know anything. If the government has done it, so it must be good."* She has had no access to any family planning services and workers. Otherwise she appeared quite receptive to such potential messages. She is clearly a woman whose contraceptive needs are "unmet" and so she becomes liable to disqualification under the law and not able to make an informed reproductive choice.

Mewaram, aged 35 years, belongs to the Rawat caste of OBC. He owns 25 bighas of land in his village in Ajmer district, Rajasthan. His annual income is about Rs.20,000. He has learnt reading and writing in adult literacy classes. He wanted to contest the Panchayat elections in 2000 and filed his nomination papers for the post of Panch. The villagers also encouraged him to contest and he won the election. He was sincere and took active part in the developmental activities of the village.

Mewaram is now an aggrieved person as he has been disqualified because his third child was born after the cut-off date of November, 1995. Mewaram had received a notice from the

Divisional Commissioner about six months back. He says that the notice was the result of jealousy and complaint by his rivals who had lost the election. His rivals had reported the matter to the Collector, who instituted an enquiry into this complaint against him.

On receiving notice he filed a petition through an advocate of Jaipur. He had no inclination to do so as he had no money to fight his case. But an ex-Sarpanch of the Srinagar Gram Panchayat who knew his case helped him fight his case on condition that Mewaram would pay the lawyer's fee if he won the case. Mewaram pleaded in the court that his third son was born on 18 April, 1994. He had the horoscope of his third son, which he showed to the interviewing team. It appeared to be a genuine one. He also produced the ration-card to the inquiry officer, in which the age of the child was recorded. He claims that his third son was eight years old (on August, 2001) and was studying in Class II in the primary school in the village. This was corroborated by a local NGO representative also.

But Mewaram finally lost his case and was disqualified in July, 2001. He contends that he had limited the size of his family to three and got his wife sterilised under the family planning programme. So he was anguished by the disqualification and said that this law is a blow to the poor who have been given an opportunity of reservations in the Panchayats. He cited the cases of a woman Panch of his Gram Panchayat, and two male Panches who are also poor and have met the same fate. He said, *"Why is the government proclaiming that reservation has been provided for the downtrodden in the Panchayats to bring them up. It is to meet this fate for a poor person like me"*! Since Mewaram had no money to fight the case any further, he did not even try to move a higher court.

Mitwa, an OBC and the most educated woman in her family, was selected as a *Pradhan* of a Panchayat Samiti in Rajasthan in 1995. But the birth of her third child has been a major source of tension for her though she has tried to suppress its evidence. This young woman said that she did not want the third child, a second son, but her husband did who said that "*two sons are like two eyes*". "*We end up producing children due to men, women are not to be blamed,*" she says. She had three abortions after the election. She showed visible signs of tension when we met her first as a working Pradhan, since, as a lactating mother, she could not openly feed her undeclared child or take it to meetings.

She continued until 1998, when she was disqualified for violation of the two-child law. As soon as she had the third childbirth, the Up-pradhan of the Panchayat Samiti made a complaint against her. She contested the case and did not really consider getting out of the post as she tried to tell the field team in her interview. She had claimed in the court that she had only two children and that the allegation about the birth of her third child on 9 May, 1997 was not correct. She had tried to indicate that she had adopted copper-T after her second child and the third child alleged to be born to her is of her sister who is married in the same family. Finally the court ruled that she had the third child in May, 1997 as claimed in the complaint and the judgment of August, 1998 went against her. Despite being politically connected, with knowledge about the Panchayat Raj system and a new woman entrant to Panchayat wanting to work, her functioning was clearly impaired by the tense state of her mind. Her agonising experience of complaints and litigation has made her bitter and disillusioned.

Priti Meena is a 31 years old ST Sarpanch of a Gram Panchayat in Jaipur district of Rajasthan. She was educated up to Class VIII and was also working as an Anganwari worker. Her husband is a post-graduate but presently looking after his agricultural lands. She still claimed during our field work that she had gone for sterilization in 1996 to limit her family size. Her own appointment as an Anganwari worker, her mother as a field worker, her ability to go to the High Court twice in this case and get stay orders show that she and the family are quite resourceful.

She admitted that within two-three months of her becoming a Sarpanch a complaint was made that she had an additional child after November, 1995. She described how she had to repeatedly go to the Panchayat Samiti office in connection with this inquiry and how she was removed on 20 September, 2000 but she went to the High Court where within four days she got a stay order and in these four days the charge of the post was not given to anyone else. She still says that the child she is supposed to have given birth after 1995 is of her brother-in-law. She refers to this as the conspiracy of the Upsarpanch and her opponents.

In this case, a complaint was made that she had contested the election by giving wrong information about the number of children as she had more than two children. She did not file any reply but obtained a stay of these proceedings from the Rajasthan High Court. Thereafter on the pleading of the state government, the High Court cancelled the stay order and directed the inquiry to be completed in four months. The Sarpanch again did not give any reply but the records, namely, sterilization certificate and records of the MCH (Maternity and Child Health) services were seen in the inquiry, which showed that she had her fourth child in July, 1997 and she had contested the Panchayat election by stating wrong facts.

The 50 years old Raigar (SC), Upsarpanch of this Gram Panchayat had filed the complaint against her. He was the Sarpanch from 1981 to 1984. His 45 years old illiterate wife is a Panch in this Panchayat. They have five children. He says that the Sarpanch's fourth child was born in July, 1997. She is also an Anganwari worker and had taken 15 days' leave at that time. He confirmed that he had complained against her.

Another Meena woman Panch of this Panchayat, who is 45 years old and has eight children, says that she had conducted the delivery of the Sarpanch's two older children. She does not know where the Sarpanch had delivered her younger children but she had seen her when she was pregnant. The Sarpanch, on the other hand, insists that the child is not hers but is of her husband's younger brother.

Those who conducted the inquiry told us that there were two sets of records of the family planning operation of the Sarpanch, and the ANM's record is also tampered with. The birth and death register also does not have the name of the child. The child's entry is also not there in the pulse polio register. The child's father's name in the ration-card is that of her brother-in-law. The Sarpanch alleges that the Up-sarpanch started the complaint of the two-child norm violation after she had moved for his disqualification for being absent in five meetings.

At the time of the field work the complaint, allegations and counter allegations and the dispute were continuing and the Sarpanch was in the post with the High Court's stay order. The issue of violation of the norm has become only a tool to harass or oust one's rivals. Neither party to the dispute seems to be concerned about the size of their own family or of their opponent or about stopping to reflect about the reason for introducing this eligibility clause. The irony of the situation of the complainant and other Panches supporting this complaint having five and eight children respectively is lost on everyone.

Ram Kunwar, a thirty years old well-placed Rajput Sarpanch from Sawai Madhopur district in Rajasthan, was educated upto Class IX and came from a reasonably well-off agricultural family. Her father-in-law had been a Sarpanch for 18 years. So she contested for the post of Sarpanch. She had one son and two daughters. The family wanted one more son since one son is equal to only one eye. So she had her fourth child a daughter when she was the Sarpanch. Being aware of the two-child norm in the Panchayat, she took admission for this delivery in a hospital in another city and that too in her sister-in-law's name. After a baby girl was born she left the infant behind in town to avoid detection but it died at the age of six months, reportedly of "rickets".

She faced an inquiry due to a complaint in respect of this violation of the two-child norm. The Panchayat Samiti as well as the Zila Parishad carried out a probe as the villagers complained. She admitted that she had a lot of problems for five-six months when the enquiry officer visited and recorded her statement and also of the complainant. The probe brought out that the childbirth was in a hospital in Jaipur but the certificate of the hospital did not have the correct name. So the complaint against her got dropped. The husband smugly told the field team that the complainants could only bring a wrong birth certificate. The villagers on the other hand were certain that the Sarpanch had delivered a baby.

The husband also has a second wife, a nurse, who has two children. The neglect of the female child and her death have been the price to pay for the woman Sarpanch to stay on in the post to keep the family's hold on the Panchayat. She found nothing wrong in her husband's second marriage. She spoke about how well connected she was with her affinal family member who was a senior government official and how she was able to tell the inquiry officer that the baby girl had died and how the villagers were not able to prove anything and how she continued in her post.

She had a fourth child as the family wanted one more son. She was aware of the law but the risk of disqualification for violation of the norm did not deter her or the family. They only resorted to the practice of wrong name in hospital, neglect of the girl child, using connections to see that the inquiry was closed and she completed her tenure. The law's operation has had no effect on the fertility decision but has contributed to the girl child's neglect and death.

Rasulan Chita, a 45 years old OBC, illiterate, is Sarpanch of a Gram Panchayat in Ajmer district in Rajasthan. She is the second wife of Rana who already had a first living wife who had five children, all dead. He left her and brought Rasulan under *nata* (traditional common law marriage). The couple is poor. They have a small piece of land and are wage workers. They migrated to Haryana for nine years and worked on construction sites. In the meantime they had three children—two daughters and one son. In the 1995 election, Rasulan became a Ward Panch. In the same year, her 14 years old son died of snakebite. The daughters were already married. Hence Rana brought another wife under *nata.* In between Rasulan became pregnant and he then left the other woman whom he had brought under *nata.*

In July, 1996 she had a premature delivery of a baby girl who died within one night, but the family claims that it was a stillbirth. Some people feel that pre-natal sex determination test was done and, as it was a female foetus, there was induced abortion. Despite this no complaint was made against Rasulan. She again contested in the February, 2000 election in which three other women including one former Sarpanch supporter also contested. The son of this other candidate had objected to Rasulan's nomination form on the ground of her having a third child. The returning officer conducted an enquiry in the village, recorded statements of people and with Rasulan's affidavit permitted her to contest election. She won the election and so 15 days later her opponent filed a petition against her in which the allegation of the third child was raised and the supporting document was the ANM's record about the birth of a female child in July, 1996.

The ANM told us that her register had only an entry of Rasulan's pregnancy and no record about the birth or death of a female baby and that she had not given any certificate to the other party but Rasulan and her husband feel that she has given the certificate to the other party calculating nine-month pregnancy and this certificate has been filed in the court. Thus this claim, they say, is legally wrong. They have complained to the Collector and requested for the ANM's transfer. The court gave a stay on Rasulan's acting as a Sarpanch. Then Rasulan engaged a lawyer and got the stay vacated. A case is going on in the civil court. For this case, Ahmedi, a 61 years old woman, and her son and the former Sarpanch are responsible. The complainants had also tried to have a compromise with Rasulan and her husband but no such compromise had taken place so far.

Two inferences are clear from this case. A woman from a family which is basically wage worker has tried to enter the Panchayat and then continue but these efforts are being stymied by local politics and a former Sarpanch's influence. She and her husband, on the other hand, have perhaps gone for a pre-natal sex determination test and have gone for induced abortion since it was a female foetus. They had obviously gone for pregnancy to have a son. These are serious implications for any policy or objective of women's empowerment and their entry in political institutions. The cases of foeticide to avoid disqualification or to limit the family size but to continue pregnancy in case of sex determination test reporting a male foetus show the continuation of the overriding desire for a son.

5

Outcomes, Conclusions and Emerging Issues

ANALYSIS OF OUTCOMES

Framework of Analysis

The two-child norm for elected offices was recommended by the committee on population set up by the National Development Council as a result of its concern for the high population growth rate defined after the 1991 Census. It was stated that it would show that the government was serious about this problem. The assumption was that this norm would check the high population growth rate which, in turn, would lead to improved development indicators and a better quality of life for the citizens of India. It was incorporated in the Panchayat related laws in different states with the assumption that Panchayat leaders with two children would serve as role models for the rest of the community.

These assumptions and compulsions have to be balanced against the aspirational goals and Constitutional commitments which the Indian State has for its citizens. Since this norm was introduced in the Panchayats almost simultaneously with the entry of women and weaker sections with the 73rd Amendment, it is important to see if this norm furthers or negates the objectives of this Amendment. Thus based on our study we try to answer a set of very simple questions. These are:

(a) Is the two-child norm as a condition for eligibility to hold elected Panchayat posts necessary for development and population stabilisation?

(b) Are the Constitutional goals of equality of opportunity for women and the backward sections of society safeguarded with the adoption of this norm in the context of the Panchayats?
(c) Is the two-child norm leading to greater adoption of family planning practices?
(d) Can the adoption of the two-child norm lead to the adoption of any practices that are harmful for the status of women?
(e) Can the adoption of the two-child norm support or negate the goal of the 73rd Constitutional Amendment?

Background Characteristics of the Five States and the Need of the Two-Child Norm

The introduction of the two-child norm in the Panchayats evolved in somewhat similar ways in all the five states. The 73rd Amendment to the Constitution of India made it mandatory for all states to review their existing Panchayat laws and to make them in conformity with its provisions. Some of the states used this opportunity to incorporate the two-child norm. Rajasthan had already included the norm in its Panchayat law even before this revision. Madhya Pradesh provides a substantially different experience as the two-child norm was introduced well after the new Panchayat law was enacted after the Constitutional Amendment. In fact, it was introduced very soon after two rounds of Panchayat elections under the new law and without any debate or study of the experience of states where it had been introduced in 1993 and 1994. What is equally interesting is that the two-child norm and the state population policy were being formulated in this state at around the same time.

The Constitution of India, the National Population Policy, the National Policy on the Empowerment of Women, India's ratification of the Convention on Elimination of All Forms of Discrimination Against Women (CEDAW) taken together provide substantial evidence of India's commitment to improving the status of women and achieving gender equality. The concept of human development is slowly replacing economic development as the main purpose of progress. Population growth trends show that the rate of growth has slowed, though the 'momentum' effect continues to be substantial.

The background characteristics of the five states (Table 2.3) reveal that in two of the five states, namely, Andhra Pradesh and Orissa, the population growth rate is quite low and certainly not the cause for any panic. In two states the contraceptive prevalence is high. In four states the rate of increase of contraceptive prevalence in the five years between the NFHS I and II was substantially more than the national average. In Madhya Pradesh, which did not fall into any of the above categories the unmet need for contraception was nearly one in every six couples. These characteristics show that the two-child norm as a condition for Panchayat posts cannot be necessary for development and population stabilisation.

In gender *related* data (Table 2.4) four states emerge with concerns regarding the status of women either due to the high literacy gap between men and women or even the more disquieting fact of declining child sex ratio. Given these circumstances the risk of the already precarious status of *women* being adversely affected through the application of the coercive law of the norm is high.

Haryana has the best overall development indicators with the highest net state domestic product, and the highest human development index rank among the five states. But the state scores the least in the decline in the sex ratio and particularly the child sex ratio and thus is a high-risk state in terms of the potential of the norm affecting the status of women. In Madhya Pradesh and Orissa the proportion of people living below the poverty line is as high as 37 per cent and 47 per cent. These two states also have a substantial tribal population. Hence, the potential of the two-child norm affecting the poor and tribal women has to be kept in mind. In short an examination of the background information relating to population, development and women's status indicates that the application of the norm has the potential to harm the status of women or is unnecessary in all the five states even if it is assumed that such a norm enforced by law can be effective in influencing fertility decisions.

An analysis of the number of cases of disqualification on the ground of violation of the two-child norm in the state of Madhya Pradesh and in its different districts between November, 2001 and June, 2004 and the trend of child sex ratio there reinforces this apprehension further.[1] A number of districts, e.g., Bhind, Morena, Gwalior, Sheopur, Datia and Guna, which have an adverse and declining sex ratio and child sex ratio have reported none or very few cases of disqualification despite their known higher political awareness and rivalries which prompt individuals to complain against their rivals. While the number of disqualification cases is affected by a number of factors, there is naturally an apprehension that disqualification is being avoided and evaded here by sex selection tests and female foeticide. On the other hand, some of the districts with a better child sex ratio and the trend of increase or small decline between 1991–2001, e.g., Shivpuri, Seoni, Tikamgarh, Rewa, Vidisha show a larger number of disqualification cases. This, of course, will need further in-depth study.

Impact on the Status of Women

The two-child norm has an adverse impact on the status of women. *Women face double-edged challenge*—decision-making on reproduction has not been in women's hands and yet they suffer directly (as candidates) or indirectly (as spouse of those disqualified) the consequences of implementation of the norm. Some reported cases of induced abortions and attempted abortions were linked with stopping the birth of a girl child as the third/ additional offspring whereas having a son was seen as far outweighing the benefits of being a Panchayat representative.

A number of disquieting trends were visible in the practices used to meet the conditionalities of the law without changes in the decision about the family size and without moving away from the strong son preference. One important area of concern was the desertion of women. Other practices noted were:

- Hospital admission for delivery under wrong name, neglect and death of female infant.

- Cases of desertion and bigamy.
- Cases of pre-natal sex determination and induced abortion of female foetus.
- Husband seeking abortion of wife's pregnancy when it was at an advanced stage.
- Children given away for adoption, leading to the forcible separation of the mother and her child.
- Allegations of infidelity, denial of paternity of the third child.
- Women exposed to violence from their opponents which included physical and psychological violence and then followed by complaint of violation of the two-child norm.

These practices have serious implications for the status of women.

Impact on Adoption of Contraception/Small Family Norm

Our study highlights some very significant issues which need to be considered when examining the assumption whether the two-child norm for Panchayat leaders can help set a social acceptance of the small family norm. Overall a large proportion (76 per cent) of the disqualified representatives were practising contraception (53 per cent permanent methods and 23 per cent others). This had little to do with their preference of family size. The desire for a small family existed independent of this law, but when it was a choice between leadership position and family size, especially if it pertained to a son, the desire for a child won in many cases.

Since the study focused on the candidates who had faced disqualification, it was not possible to determine whether the norm did indeed lead to other couples deciding to opt for a smaller than desired family. But it is significant to note that when the respondents, who expressed ignorance about the law till action was initiated against them, were asked what they would have done had they known about the new law, they did not say that they would not have had the additional child. On the contrary, they asserted that they would not have contested the election. It was also disquieting to learn that a number of disqualified representatives had resorted to induced abortion. There is a possibility that the incidence of sex selection test and induced abortions could be higher among those who did not face disqualification. As we have noted, the report of no cases of disqualification in some of the districts in MP with a very adverse child sex ratio and with high political consciousness reinforces this possibility and needs to be studied further.

Impact on Participation of Women and Dalits in Governance

The examination of state-level data from Haryana shows that nearly three-fourths of all disqualifications were because of the two-child norm. The data collected for disqualifications between 2000 and 2004 shows that in Madhya Pradesh, Chhattisgarh (carved out of Madhya Pradesh) and Rajasthan 54 per cent, 68 per cent and 63 per cent respectively of all disqualifications were for violation of the two-child norm. In Haryana these were 87 per cent.

Studies of Panchayats and women's presence and experience in the Panchayats have shown a large entry of the poor, even illiterate and younger women. Our study noted a disproportionately high number of women (41 per cent) among our respondents who were faced with disqualification for violating the two-child norm. Among the Dalits this proportion of women becomes even higher (50 per cent). The fact that most disqualification notices are issued only after third-party complaints makes the application of this norm less than evenhanded in actual practice. The democratic rights of the poor, of the backward and of women are bound to be further compromised by their vulnerability to complaints and their inability to go in for protracted and expensive litigation.

The 73rd Amendment is aimed at providing women and Dalits and younger persons an opportunity to participate in politics and governance. There was evidence in our study of women getting discouraged in view of long drawn-out court cases, inquiries and mental trauma resulting from the dilemma between continuing in the post and a simultaneous desire and family pressure for a son or a larger family. The mental trauma was noted especially in

Rajasthan where the norm has been in place for some time. This defeats the intent of the 73rd Amendment, which attempts to facilitate and encourage entry of women across class and caste into Panchayats.

The experience shows the potential of using the two-child norm to harass opponents. There was also an indication that the norm could be circumvented and evaded through manipulations which are easier for those with political or financial clout. The process of complaints, inquiry and disqualification is a continuing process encroaching upon the resources of the competent authorities and also distracting the aggrieved persons from more productive development work. The majority of the respondents felt that the legislation had been discriminatory because of its selective application to local bodies, i.e. Gram Panchayats and urban bodies and that the norm has worked against the weaker sections who of late were coming forward to contest, particularly at the Gram Panchayat level, after the 73rd Constitutional Amendment.

Conclusions and Emerging Issues

Our study clearly demonstrated that the application of the two-child norm has the potential of adversely affecting both the democratic rights and reproductive choices of individuals. It has serious consequences for the status of women. There is, however, an overwhelming public opinion, especially among the key actors like policy-makers and programme implementers, doctors and lawyers, that the norm is necessary to reduce the family size and population growth rate and give the desired impetus to development. For the officials responsible for enforcing the norm, this provision is only one of the conditions of eligibility, verified only if a candidature is objected to on that ground at the time of filing of nomination for an election or when a complaint is made. For the state officials responsible for programmes in the area of health, family welfare, etc., this norm in the Panchayats is not a major issue to be addressed by them.

Policy makers expected the two-child norm to make people

decide in favour of a small family. Their assessment was that induced abortions might be insignificant. They did not consider the norm as in any way encroaching upon the people's democratic or reproductive rights. The overall goal of "population control" is sufficient justification for harsh measures, they said. In their view, those who wanted to be in politics would definitely keep the two-child norm in view as the Sarpanch and Panch are prestigious posts and if they were disqualified because of having more children, others might learn to limit their families. They did not note that in rural India the Panchayat post is quite often taken as coming to the family and not merely to the individual family members concerned. Therefore, as we saw in Haryana, when the young woman got disqualified, an older member in the family was elected. These officials maintained that the new generation was now aware and those who wanted to contest the election would definitely take note of the norm.

Discussions with a cross-section of the population revealed two broad strands of thoughts: (1) those working at the policy level and mostly in the urban milieu supported the two-child norm; (2) the grassroot workers closer to the ground realities had doubts about its efficacy. Also, in several cases, opinions were formed on the basis of personal characteristics rather than on an in-depth understanding and long-term implications if the norm were to be followed through. Panchayat representatives, who were educated, economically relatively better off and had small families, strongly supported the norm.

People in relatively privileged positions and not directly affected by the two-child norm had either not thought about it seriously or favoured the norm to have an impact on the family size of the poor and the illiterate persons. For many it was not a preventive act, but a way to send the message advocating a small family norm. Proponents of such a view, however, seem to have missed the point that the norm itself could be a coercive measure and when legally enforced could encroach upon the democratic and reproductive rights and choices of individuals and that awareness/education, access to health and other developmental activities could have been better options. There was inadequate appreciation of the distinction between an informed responsible choice for a small family and the state's responsibility to facilitate such a choice by social development and access to quality services, on the one hand, and the coercion inherent in an externally imposed norm through a law, its limitations and negative impacts, on the other.

State Responsibility vs. Individual Responsibility

The imposition of a two-child norm by law before the state ensures provision of accessible, affordable, equitable, quality health and family welfare services ignores state's primary responsibility to provide these services. The inadequacy of these services is seen in the high unmet contraceptive needs among the desiring couples (documented by NFHS II), high unwanted fertility levels due to high IMR and poor quality health care services. The social context of early marriages, early pregnancies and son preference is also ignored and all the responsibility is placed only on the individuals, particularly women, with serious consequences for them.

Norm is Contradictory

The two-child norm not only contradicts the rights-based approach to women's development, but also the objectives of the Constitutional Amendment enacted to ensure greater political participation and empowerment of politically and socially marginalised groups of weaker sections and women. Those who had the power, influence and resources – human and financial – to manoeuvre, could circumvent the norm. It thus becomes exclusionary, particularly of those at the lower end of the caste and class hierarchy and discourages women from participating in the grassroots decentralised governance through Panchayat Raj institutions. The manner in which fertility decisions are impacted by the norm is not in keeping with the client-oriented spirit of the National Population Policy or the rights-orientation articulated in the Plan of Action of the International Conference on Population and Development 1994.

No Evidence to show that the Norm has achieved the Intended Outcome

The law was introduced with the expectations that the Panchayat representative by following the norm would be able to set an example for others to follow. Our field-based qualitative study found no corroborative evidences to this effect. On the other hand, there were enough evidences to suggest that the unintended outcomes were far more serious. Contrary to the expectation, none of the respondents had accepted contraceptives because of the norm. They adopted family planning only after the desired family size (invariably including at least one son) was achieved. Clearly, long-term familial security far outweighed political aspirations, thus defeating the very purpose of imposing the norm. Cases were noted where persons resorted to abortions particularly of female foetus. It thus has a strong potential to further aggravate the declining child sex ratio.

Weaker Sections More Vulnerable

First and foremost, disqualification hinges upon the birth of a third/additional child after a stipulated date. Manipulation and misrepresentation of date of birth are common and there were many instances of disputing the age or date of birth of the last born child, tampering with records and evidence of procuring false certificates, collusion with local officials and getting stay orders, etc.

All the scheduled caste, scheduled tribe and backward caste respondents were of the view that the two-child norm was essentially used for settling political scores. Some felt that the norm had to be located in broader structural constraints within which people operate. A Dalit activist in Nalgonda district said:

"... In Dalit culture a man with one son is called 'one-eyed fellow' so most Dalits prefer to have more than one son. This is the Dalits' lifestyle... [It is because] health care is not within the reach of the Dalits and the infant mortality rate is high."

Another Dalit contestant who was facing trial for violating the two-child norm questioned the applicability of the norm only to the lower rungs of political hierarchy and asked why it was not being extended to cover those contesting for member of parliament or member of legislative assembly. According to him, propertied castes could have as many children as they wanted, while those poorly off went in for sterilization on their own. He said that he was not contesting any more elections.

What becomes very clear is that the two-child norm gets selectively applied to persons depending upon their socio-economic vulnerability, political rivalries, perceived importance of the post occupied and as a tool to discourage potentially promising candidates. At the same time, those who had to face disqualification or were finally disqualified had used various ways ranging from misrepresenting and/or hiding facts about the number of children to deserting/divorcing wives to avoid being implicated. In doing so, women's reproductive rights have been seriously encroached upon.

These negative consequences were, on the one hand, without attaining any of the intended outcomes of the two-child norm. On the other, the two-child norm is seen to be having a dampening effect on those lower in the caste and class hierarchy, particularly women, in terms of discouraging them from participating in grassroots-level institutions of governance.

Need for a Wider Debate on the Rationale of the Two-Child Norm

One issue for concern that emerged related to the lack of awareness among the key members of society, which includes doctors, lawyers, policy-makers and civil servants, about the linkages between population and development as well as the fact that India is currently going through a "population momentum" phase. The concept of "Population Explosion" still seems to be the dominant discourse even though it has been discarded in favour of "population stabilization" and "human development". All efforts have to be made to educate key urban influential persons through diverse media articles and so on.

The issues need to be debated in the context of grassroots reality, the equity oriented focus of the Indian Constitution and the adverse and demeaning practices for women resulting from the implementation of this norm. The entire question of the unproven efficacy of an externally imposed norm that is inherently coercive when seen from the perspective of informed choice and reproductive rights and its unintended negative consequences documented in the experiences of the affected persons, on the one hand, and the perspectives of informed and reproductive rights on the other must be widely debated.

Need to Withdraw/Impose a Moratorium on the Two-child Norm Law

In the absence of any data that the norm is providing the advantages that it is supposed to have, and in the light of the adverse impacts for women and the unequal burden on the marginalised sections of society that our study has brought to light, there is a need for the central government to advise the states to either withdraw the norm or impose a moratorium on its implementation.

This norm imposed by a law must be withdrawn in the interest of women and weaker sections, their participation in grassroots institutions and in view of the negative implications for woman and girl children seen in the experiences of those affected by this law. There is also no evidence that it has the impact on fertility decisions assumed in introducing it. On the other hand, there is enough evidence that a desire for smaller families and contraceptives already exists independent of this law. The state has to focus on social development, supporting women's agency and universal availability of quality health and family welfare services.

NOTES

1. The districts of Morena (child sex ratio 837), Bhind (child sex ratio 832), Datia (child sex ratio 874), Gwalior (child sex ratio 853) with sharp decline in child sex ratio (number of females for 1000 male in 0-6 age group) from 1991 to 2001 have reported no case of persons disqualified for violation of the two-child norm up to 2004.

Appendices

APPENDIX 1

The Andhra Pradesh Panchayat Raj Act, 1994

Section 19. Disqualification of Candidates

××× ××× ×××

(3) A person having more than two children shall be disqualified for election or for continuing as member:

Provided that the birth within one year from the date of commencement of the Andhra Pradesh Panchayat Raj Act, 1994 hereinafter in this clause referred to as the date of such commencement, of an additional child shall not be taken into consideration for the purposes of this clause:

Provided further that a person having more than two children (excluding the child if any born within one year from the date of such commencement) shall not be disqualified under this clause for so long as the number of children he had on the date of such commencement does not increase:

Provided also that the Government may direct that the disqualification in this section shall not apply in respect of a person for reasons to be recorded in writing.

Section 20. Disqualification of Members

××× ××× ×××

Subject to the provisions of Section 22, a member shall cease to hold office as such if he,—

(a) is or becomes subject to any of the disqualifications specified in Section 19;

Section 156. Disqualifications

××× ××× ×××

(2) The provisions of Sections — 19, 20, — shall apply to a member of the Mandal Parishad as they apply to a member of the Gram Panchayat ———

Section 184. Disqualifications

××× ××× ×××

(2) The provisions of Sections — 19, 20, — shall apply to a member of the Zila Parishad as they apply to a member of the Gram Panchayat ——

APPENDIX 2

The Haryana Panchayat Raj Act, 1994

Section 51. Suspension and Removal of Sarpanch or Panch

(3) The Director or the Deputy Commissioner concerned may, after such enquiry as he may deem fit and after giving an opportunity of being heard to a Sarpanch or [*****] a Panch, as the case may be, ask him to show cause against the action proposed to be taken against him, and by order remove him from his office...

××× ××× ×××

(b) If he was disqualified to be a member of the Gram Panchayat at the time of his election;

(c) If he incurs any of the disqualifications mentioned in section 175 after his election as member of the Gram Panchayat;

Section 175. (1) No person shall be a Sarpanch or a Panch of a Gram Panchayat or a member of a Panchayat Samiti or Zila Parishad or continue as such who—

××× ××× ×××

(q) has more than two living children.

Provided that a person having more than two children on or upto the expiry of one year of the commencement of this Act, shall not be deemed to be disqualified.

Section 177. (1) If any member of a Gram Panchayat Samiti or Zila Parishad:

(a) Who is elected as such, was subject to any of the

disqualifications mentioned in Section 175 at the time of his election.

(b) During the term for which he has been elected, incurs any of the disqualifications mentioned in Section 175.

shall be disqualified from continuing to be a member and his office shall become vacant.

APPENDIX 3

The Madhya Pradesh Panchayat Avam Gram Swaraj Adhiniyam, 1993

Section 36. Disqualification for being office bearer of Panchayat

××× ××× ×××

1. (m) has more than two living children one of whom is born on or after the 26th day of January, 2001.
   *Inserted by The Madhya Pradesh Panchayat Raj (Sanshodhan) Adhiniyam (MP 14 of 2000) with effect from 26-01-2001.
2. If any person having been elected as an office-bearer of Panchayat:
   (a) subsequently becomes subject to any of the disqualifications mentioned in sub-section (1) ————.
   he shall——cease to be such office bearer and his office shall become vacant.
3. In every case the authority competent to decide whether a vacancy has occurred under sub-section (2) shall be Collector in respect of Gram Panchayat and Janpad Panchayat and Commissioner in respect of Zila Parishad who may give his decision either on an application made to him by any person or on his own motion —————.

APPENDIX 4-A

The Orissa Zila Parishad Act, 1991

Section 33. Disqualifications for becoming a member and continuing as member

(1) A person shall not be eligible to stand for election under clause (a) of sub-section (1) of Section 6, if he—

××× ××× ×××

(w) has more than two children;

××× ××× ×××

Provided further that the disqualification under clause (w) shall not apply to a person who has more than two children on the date of commencement of the Orissa Zila Parishad (Amendment) Act, 1993 or, as the case may be, within a period of one year of such commencement, unless he begets an additional child after the said period of one year.

* Inserted by OGE No. 1189 dated 1-9-1993.

Section 34. District Judge to decide question of disqualification

1. Whenever it is alleged that any member of a Parishad is or has become disqualified, or whenever any such member is himself in doubt whether or not he is or has become disqualified, such member or any other member may, and the President at the request of the Parishad shall, apply to the District Judge, having jurisdiction over the place where the office of the Parishad is situated, for a decision on the allegation or doubt.

APPENDIX 4-B

The Orissa (Panchayat Samiti) Act, 1959

Section 45. Disqualification for becoming a member and continuing as member

[1] A person shall not be eligible to stand for election [under sub-sections (1) of Section 16 if he:

××× ××× ×××

(v) has more than two children:

××× ××× ×××

Provided further that the disqualification under clause (v) shall not apply to a person who has more than two children on the date of commencement of the Orissa Panchayat Samiti (Amendment) Act, 1994 or, as the case may be, within a period of one year of such commencement, unless he begets an additional child after the said period of one year.

* Inserted by Orissa Act 7 of 1994.

Section 45B. District Judge to decide question of disqualification

1. Whenever it is alleged that any member of a Samiti is or has become disqualified or whenever any such member is himself in doubt whether or not he is or has become disqualified such member or any other member may, and the Chairman at the request of Samitis, shall, apply to the District Judge, having jurisdiction over the place where the office of the Samiti is situated, for a decision on the allegation or doubt.

APPENDIX 4-C

The Orissa Gram Panchayat Act, 1965

Section 25. Disqualification for membership of Gram Panchayat

(1) A person shall be disqualified for being elected or nominated as a Sarpanch or any other member of the Gram Panchayat constituted under this Act, if he:

××× ××× ×××

(v) has more than two children:

Provided that the disqualification under Clause (v) shall not apply to any person who has more than two children on the date of commencement of the Orissa Gram Panchayats (Amendment) Act, 1994 or, as the case may be, within a period of one year of such commencement, unless he begets an additional child after the said period of one year.

* Inserted by Orissa Act of 1994 with effect from 22-4-1994.

Section 26. Procedure of giving effect to disqualifications

1. Whenever it is alleged that any Sarpanch or Naib-Sarpanch or any other member is or has become disqualified or whenever any such person is himself in doubt whether or not he is or has become so disqualified such person or any other member may, and the Sarpanch at the request of the Gram Panchayat shall apply to the Collector for a decision on the allegation of doubt.
2. The Collector may *suo motu,* or on receipt of an application under Sub-section (1), ××× determine whether or not such a person is or has become disqualified and make an order in that behalf which shall be final and conclusive.

APPENDIX 5

The Rajasthan Panchayat Raj Act, 1994
(As amended w.e.f. 23-4-1994)

Section 19. Qualifications for election as a Panch or a Member

Every person registered as a voter in the list of voters of a Panchayat Raj Institution shall be qualified for election as a Panch or, as the case may be, a member of such Panchayat Raj Institution unless such person:

××× ××× ×××

*(l) has more than two children:
Provided that:

××× ××× ×××

(iv) The birth during the period from the date of commencement of this Act, hereinafter in this proviso referred to as the date of such commencement, to 27th November, 1995, of an additional child shall not be taken into consideration for the purpose of the disqualification mentioned in clause (1) and a person having more than two children (excluding the child, if any, born during the period from the date of such commencement to 27th November, 1995) shall not be disqualified under that clause for so long as the number of children he had on the date of commencement of this Act does not increase.

Explanation – For the purpose of clause (1) of Section 19, where the couple has only one child from the earlier delivery or deliveries on the date of commencement of this Act and thereafter, any number of children born out of single subsequent delivery shall be deemed to be one entity.

---

* Substituted w.e.f. 23-4-1994 by an amendment in 1995.

Glossary

ADM: Additional District Magistrate.

ANM : Auxiliary Nurse Midwife.

Angawari Workers: Workers running Anganwari Cetre, a centre for giving package of services to children 0-6 years in ICDS projects.

BC: Backward Caste.

BDO: Block Development Officer.

CMO: Chief Medical Officer.

CPR: Couple Protection Rate.

Deputy Commissioner/Collector: The administrative head and incharge of administration of the district.

Gram Panchayat (G.P.): A Panchayat for a village or group of villages—the lowest tier of the three-tier Panchayat structure.

ICDS: Integrated Child Development Services.

Janpad Panchayat: A Panchayat at the block level in M.P.

Mandal Parishad: A Panchayat at the intermediate level Mandal in Andhra Pradesh.

MLA: Member of Legislative Assembly.

MP: Member of Parliament

Panch: Member of a village Panchayat.

Panchayat Samiti: A Panchayat at the block level which is the intermediate level of the Panchayat structure.

PHC: Primary Health Centre.

Sarpanch: Chairperson of a village Panchayat.

SC: Scheduled Caste.

SDM: Sub-Divisional Magistrate.

SHG: Self Help Group.

TFR: Total Fertility Rate.

VAO: Village Administrative Officer.

Zamindar: Landlord.

Zila Parishad/Zila Panchayat: A Panchayat at the district level, the top tier of the Panchayat structure.

References

Anagnost, Ann (1995). A surfeit of Bodos: Population and the Rationality of the state in Post-Mao China. In Faye D. Ginsburg and Rapp Rayna (eds.). *Conceiving the New World Order: The Global Politics of Reproduction*. University of California Press, Berkeley, Los Angeles, London.

Bhat, P.N. Mari (2003). Two Child Norm: In Defence of Supreme Court Judgement. *Economic and Political Weekly,* November, 2001.

CWDS (1997). National Population Policy—*Perspectives from the Women's Movement, Compilation of Documents,* Centre for Women's Development Studies, New Delhi.

Greenhalgh, Susan (2001). Fresh Winds in Beijing: Chinese Feminists Speak Out on the One Child Policy and Women's Lives. SIGNS: *Journal of Women in Culture and Society*, 20 (3): 601-41. SIGNS, 847-886.

Government of India, (2000). *National Population Policy 2000*, Ministry of Health and Family Welfare, New Delhi.

ICPD Programme of Action (1994). UNFPA, *Report of the International Conference on Population and Development,* Cairo, 5-13 September.

Mohan Rao (2003). Two Child Norm in Panchayats: Many Steps Back, *Economic and Political Weekly*, August 16.

Sen, Amartya (1995). Population Policy: Authoritarianism versus Cooperation – Lecture delivered on August 17, 1995, New Delhi – *International Lecture Series on Population Issues*.

Short, Susan E. and Zhai Fengying (1998). Looking Locally at China's One-child Policy, *Studies in Family Planning*; 29,4: 373-387.

Zeng Yi: (1989) "Is the Chinese Family Planning Program 'tightening up'?" *Population and Development Review* 15, 2: 333-337.

Index